GODS, GODDESSES,
AND MYTHS
OF CREATION

GODS, GODDESSES, AND MYTHS OF CREATION

A Thematic Source Book of the History of Religions

Part 1 of *FROM PRIMITIVES TO ZEN*

MIRCEA ELIADE

1817

HARPER & ROW, PUBLISHERS

NEW YORK, EVANSTON, SAN FRANCISCO, LONDON

ISBN: 0-06-062136-2

LIBRARY OF CONGRESS CATALOG CARD NUMBER: 73-20949

First Harper & Row paperback edition published in 1974. This book contains chapters I and II of FROM PRIMITIVES TO ZEN.

Preface to the Paperback Edition

The instigation for this anthology of religious texts and its three companion volumes came during my first years of teaching History of Religions at the University of Chicago. In discussing a specific problem, I expected my students to read at least some of the basic original sources; but I soon discovered that I was unable to recommend to them any single work where one might find a number of essential texts regarding, for example, high gods, cosmogonic myths, conceptions of death and the afterlife, etc. Although we have many source books, some of them excellent, for the most important religions, there were then no comprehensive anthologies in English presenting religious documents according to themes and topics. It seems to me that only by reading a certain number of religious texts related to the same subject (cosmogony, initiation, myths on the origin of death, etc.) is a student able to grasp their structural similarities and their differences.

Any thematic classification of religious documents implies a certain amount of arbitrariness. Some of the texts located under one classification could just as well have been integrated into another classification. But this source book is designed to be *read* first, from beginning to end, and only afterward to be *consulted*. A cross-reference index will help the reader, if he so wishes, to examine consecutively all the documents related to a specific religion or a particular cultural-geographic area such as Mesopotamia, Ancient Greece, India (or again just one segment of Indian religion: Vedism, Brahmanism, Buddhism, etc.), or the 'primitives' (but also just Australia, Oceania, Africa, Asia, North or South America).

A disturbing problem was raised by the respective proportions to be allotted to the documents representing the different religions and cultural-geographic areas. I was understandably eager to include the most representative religious texts; on the other hand, the thematic classification compelled me to illustrate all the important religious beliefs, conceptions, rituals, and institutions. Thus, for example, because I selected copiously from the *Tao Tê Ching,* the Vedic hymns, and the *Upanishads,* I was compelled to be sparing with Chinese and Indian rituals.

For obvious reasons, only a limited number of documents could be reprinted *in toto.* Omissions in the body of the text are indicated by ellipsis points. In the case of long documents, portions omitted are summarized. In rare cases, when the text was unusually long, I gave a résumé with long quotations. Explanatory notes are restricted to bare essentials; in many instances, I made use of or adapted the translator's notes. When it seemed necessary, I introduced a document or a group of documents with a brief comment. My own comments are printed in italics. Commentaries by others are printed in the same type as the documents they accompany; credit is given in the source line for the document. The use of parentheses and brackets within the documents reprinted follows the style of the book from which the particular selection was taken.

I have tried to avoid using materials from books and periodicals that are rare or hard to get. Thus the reader interested in a specific topic can find additional documents in rather easily accessible publications. The selective bibliography at the end of the volume was prepared with the same end in view: only the most useful and important books are listed. Whenever I could cite a monograph on a specific subject containing a rich and well-organized bibliography, I thought it unnecessary to quote other works.

I have made use only of existing English translations of sacred texts. In the case of Ancient Near Eastern, Indian, Greek, Chinese, and Japanese texts, I chose from all the competent translations available, in order to convey to the reader the various possibilities for rendering such abstruse and nonfamiliar texts. In selecting documents related to the 'primitive,' pre-literate societies, I followed the same principle: I limited my choice to works written in, or translated into, English. I hasten to add that although the term 'primitive' is misleading, and should be replaced by 'pre-literate' or 'archaic,' I have kept it, with the majority of authors, for reasons of convenience.

I have tried to include documents from almost all the important religious traditions, from primitive religion to the Ancient Near East to Islam, late Buddhism, and Zen. I have not included Hittite and Ugaritic texts, however, because their fragmentary condition would have demanded too extensive a commentary; furthermore, there are many readily available and competent translations of such texts. A more serious omission is that of Judaism and Christianity. But one cannot present these religions without quoting extensively from the Old and New Testaments, and it seemed unwise to increase the bulk and price of this source book considerably by reproducing such well-known texts. However, companion volumes presenting the Judaic and Christian documents on a somewhat similar thematic basis would be timely. For the moment, the omission of Judaism and Christianity may give the reader a rather inexact idea of the novelty and uniqueness of Muhammad's prophetic experience and of Islamic mystical and theological speculations on the One God. But of course I am assuming

Preface

that the majority of readers will know something of the other two older monotheistic traditions.

No author of such anthology can hope to satisfy all of his colleagues or, even less so, all of his readers. No matter how 'objective' an author may be in collecting, classifying, and presenting religious documents, his choice is ultimately a personal one. But I should like to point out that this book must be judged as a whole, and not from the particular viewpoint of the anthropologist, or the classical scholar, or the orientalist. As I have already said, the book was conceived as one to be read from beginning to end, and not merely consulted. For the same reason I have tried to limit the scientific apparatus to a minimum. I have not intended to bring out another scholarly work for the exclusive use of the scholar, but a simple and readable book accessible to any *honnête homme* curious about the religious beliefs of his fellow men.

I have to thank my friend and colleague Professor Joseph Kitagawa for helping me in the selection of Japanese materials, Mrs. Rehova Arthur for carefully typing a great portion of the manuscript, Mr. Alan Miller for reading a number of Islamic texts, and Mr. David Knipe for editing and providing notes (not otherwise credited) to the Indian and Scandinavian materials. I am grateful to Miss Nancy Auer for typing and editing most of the Mesopotamian documents, for helping me at various stages of the work, and also for reading and correcting the proofs. Finally, I am thankful to my wife not only for typing a certain number of texts, but especially for encouraging me to continue and complete this work, which kept me intermittently busy for five years. Of course, had I known that so much work would be involved, I would not have dared to embark on such a project. My one consolation for the time and energy consumed is that this source book and its three companion volumes will help the student and the interested reader to confront and understand the religious life of ancient and non-Western man.

MIRCEA ELIADE

University of Chicago

Publisher's Note to the Paperback Edition

The selections in *From Primitives to Zen* are numbered consecutively from no. 1 to no. 306. The consecutive numbering is retained in this paperback edition to facilitate the use of the cross-reference system. Nos. 1-74 are contained in *Gods, Goddesses, and Myths of Creation;* nos. 75-157 in *Man and the Sacred;* nos. 158-197 in *Death, Afterlife, and Eschatology;* nos. 198-306 in *From Medicine Men to Muhammad.*

Contents

CHAPTER I

GODS, GODDESSES, AND SUPERNATURAL BEINGS

A. DIVINITIES OF PRIMITIVES (PRE-LITERATE
    SOCIETIES)   *page* 3

   1. Australian Supernatural Beings   3

AFRICAN HIGH GODS

   2. Nzambi, the High God of the Bakongo   6
   3. The Supreme Being of the Isoko (Southern Nigeria)   6
   4. Ngai, the High God of the Kikuyu   7
   5. Leza, the High God of the Ba-ila of Northern Rhodesia   8
   6. The Supreme Being of the Herero   9
   7. Raluvhimba, the High God of the Venda   10

NORTH AMERICAN INDIANS

   8. Wakan Tanka, the Supreme Deity of the Dakota   11
   9. The 'Great Spirit' of the Lenape   12
  10. Tirawa, the Supreme God of the Pawnee   13

POLYNESIA, COLOMBIA, LABRADOR, NEW GUINEA

  11. The Maori Supreme Being (Polynesia)   14
  12. The Universal Mother and Supreme Deity (Kagaba
       people, Colombia)
  13. A South American Epiphany of the Sun God
       (Apinayé tribe, Brazil)   16
  14. The Master of the Caribou (Naskapi Indians, Labrador
       Peninsula)   18
  15. Hainuwele and the 'Creative Murder' (Ceram, New
       Guinea)   18

Contents

B. GODS OF THE ANCIENT NEAR EAST, ANCIENT INDIA,
AND JAPAN   21

16. Enki, a Sumerian High God   21
17. The Egyptian High God in the Age of the *Coffin Texts*,
    (*Coffin Texts*, 714)   24
18. Atum, a Bisexual High God (*Coffin Texts*, I, 161 ff.)   25
19. Debate between Osiris and the High God (*Book of the
    Dead*, chapter 175)   25
20. Amenhotep IV and *The Hymn to Aten*   27
21. Varuna, the All-Knowing God (*Rig Veda*, I, 25, 1-3,
    7-14)   31
22. 'King Varuna is there . . .' (*Atharva Veda*, IV, 16,
    1-6)   32
23. Varuna and Indra (*Rig Veda*, IV, 42, 1-7, 10)   33
24. 'What god shall we adore with our oblation?' (*Rig
    Veda*, X, 121, 1-10)   34
25. 'Indra—who as soon as born surpassed the gods in
    power' (*Rig Veda*, II, 12, 1-5, 13)   36
26. A Vedic Hymn to the Goddess Earth (*Atharva Veda*,
    XII, 1, selections)   37
27. Vishnu, the Cosmic God (*Vishnu Purāna*, 3, 17, 14-34)   41
28. Krishna's Epiphany (*Bhagavad Gītā*, XI, selections)   43
29. To Each Generation the Tathāgata Announces His
    Name and Declares That He Has Entered Nirvāna
    (*Saddharmapundarika*, XV, 268-72)   46
30. The Bodhisattva's Infinite Compassion (*Shikshāsa-
    muccaya*, 280-2, *Vajradhvaha-sūtra*)   48
31. The Sun Goddess Amaterasu and the Storm God,
    Susa-no-o (*Nihongi*, I, 40-5)   49

C. GREEK GODS AND HEROES, AND THE IRANIAN
   SUPREME BEING, AHURA-MAZDA   52

32. To Pythian Apollo (*The Homeric Hymns*, III, 179 ff.)   52
33. The Earth, Mother of All (*The Homeric Hymns*, XXX)   55
34. Hercules,: His Labours, His Death, His Apotheosis
    Apollodorus, *The Library*, II; IV, 8—VII, 7   56

Contents

35. Demeter and the Founding of the Eleusinian Mysteries
    (*The Homeric Hymns: To Demeter*, II, 185-299)   63

36. Zalmoxis, the God of the Getae (Herodotus, *History*,
    IV, 93-6)   66

37. Zarathustra Presents a 'Summary of the Doctrine'
    (*Gāthā:Yasna* 45)   68

38. *Gāthā* of the Choice: Zarathustra Reveals the Exemplary Choice Which Took Place at the Beginning of
    the World (*Gāthā:Yasna* 30)   70

39. The Second *Gāthā* of the Choice (*Gāthā:Yasna* 31)   72

D. ISLAM: ALLAH AND HIS PROPHET   74

40. Muhammad Speaks of Allah· 'There is no god but
    He . . .' (Koran, II, 256-9; VI, 102-3)   74

41. Allah Is All-Knowing, All-Powerful—the Creator!
    (Koran, XXVII, 61-5; XXX, 47-54; XXXV, 36-9)   75

42. Allah 'is the first and the last,' the Creator, Maker, and
    Shaper . . . He Has Knowledge of Everything
    (Koran, LVII, 1-5; LVIII, 7-8; LIX, 23-5)   77

43. Allah is Light . . . (Koran, XXIV, 34-44)   78

CHAPTER II

MYTHS OF CREATION AND OF ORIGIN

A. MYTHS OF THE CREATION OF THE WORLD   83

44. Creation by Thought (Winnebago Indians of Wisconsin)   83

45. Omaha Cosmogony: At the Beginning the World was
    in God's mind   84

46. Creation from Mere Appearance (Uitoto of Colombia,
    South America)   85

47. Io and the Maori Cosmogony   86

48. Polynesian Theogony and Cosmogony (Society Islands)   87

49. An Earth-Diver Creation Myth (Maidu Indians of
    California)   88

50. The Beginning of the World (Yauelmani Yokuts of
    California)   90

Contents

51. An African Cosmogony (Boshongo, a Central Bantu Tribe of the Lunda Cluster)   91
52. The Maya-Quiché Genesis (*Popol Vuh*, chapter 1)   92
53. Japanese Cosmogony (*Nihongi* and *Ko-ji-ki*)   94
54. Egyptian Cosmogony and Theogony (*The Book of Overthrowing Apophis*)   96
55. Mesopotamian Cosmogony (*Enuma elish*)   97
56. 'Who can say whence it all came, and how creation happened?' (*Rig Veda*, X, 129)   109
57. Indian Cosmogony (*The Laws of Manu*, I, 5-16)   111
58. The Creation of the World according to the *Upanishads*   113
59. Hesiod's Theogony and Cosmogony (*Theogony*, 116-210)   114
60. Zoroastrian Dualist Cosmogony: Ohrmazd and Ahriman (*Greater Bundahishn*, I, 18-26)   117

B. A MYTH OF BEGINNING AND END   119

61. The Scandinavian Story of Creation and a Prophecy of the End of the World (*Völuspá*)   119

C. THE CREATION OF MAN   130

62. The Creation of Woman from the Earth-Mother (Maori)   130
63. Zuñi Genesis: The Creation and Emergence of Man   130
64. God and the Five Women: A Myth of the Origin of Earth, Fire, Water and Woman, from the Thompson Indians of the North Pacific Coast   135
65. A Thompson Indian Myth of the Creation of Man   136
66. A Pawnee Emergence Myth: Mother Corn Leads the First People to the Surface of the Earth   137
67. An African Story of the Creation of Man, from the Shilluk   137

D. MYTHS OF THE ORIGIN OF DEATH   139

68. The Cast Skin: A Melanasian Myth   139
69. The Stone and the Banana: An Indonesian Myth   140

Contents

70. The Moon and Resurrection: An Australian Myth   140

71. The Cruel Bird: An Australian Myth   140

72. Maui and Hine-nui-te-po: A Polynesian Myth   142

E. MYTHS OF THE FLOOD   145

73. The Flood Narrative from the *Gilgamesh Epic*   145

74. A Myth of the Deluge from Ancient India (*Shatapatha-Brāhmana*, 1, 8, 1-6)   151

ACKNOWLEDGMENTS   155

BIBLIOGRAPHY   158

ETHNIC AND GEOGRAPHIC CROSS-REFERENCE INDEX   162

CHAPTER I

Gods, Goddesses
and Supernatural Beings

A. DIVINITIES OF PRIMITIVES
(PRE-LITERATE SOCIETIES)

1. AUSTRALIAN SUPERNATURAL BEINGS

Beliefs of tribes of Southeast Australia.

The following are the beliefs of the Kulin as they appear in their legends, and from the statements of surviving Wurunjerri to me. *Bunjil*, as represented by them, seems to be an old man, the benign *Ngurungaeta* or Headman of the tribe, with his two wives, who were *Ganawarra* (Black Swan), and his son *Binbeal*, the rainbow, whose wife was the second rainbow which is sometimes visible. *Bunjil* taught the Kulin the arts of life, and one legend states that in that time the Kulin married without any regard for kinship. Two medicine-men *(Wirrarap)* went up to him in the *Tharangalk-bek*, and he said in reply to their request that the Kulin should divide themselves into two parts— '*Bunjil* on this side and *Waang* on that side, and *Bunjil* should marry *Waang* and *Waang* marry *Bunjil*.'

Another legend relates that he [*Bunjil*] finally went up to the sky-land with all his people (the legend says his 'sons') in a whirlwind, which Bellin-bellin (the Musk-crow) let out of his skin bag at his order. There, as the old men instructed the boys, he still remains, looking down on the Kulin. A significant instance of this belief is that Berak, when a boy, 'before his whiskers grew,' was taken by his *Kangun* (mother's brother) out of the camp at night, who, pointing to the star Altair with his spear-thrower, said: 'See! that one is *Bunjil*; you see him, and he sees you.' This was before Batman settled on the banks of the Yarra River, and is conclusive as to the primitive character of this belief. . . .

Usually *Bunjil* was spoken of as *Mami-ngata*, that is 'Our Father,' instead of by the other name *Bunjil*.

It is a striking phase in the legends about him that the human element preponderates over the animal element. In fact, I cannot see any trace of the latter in him, for he is in all cases the old black-fellow, and not the eagle-hawk, which his name denotes; while another actor

3

may be the kangaroo, the spiny ant-eater, or the crane, and as much animal as human. . . .

Among the Kurnai, under the influence of the initiation ceremonies, the knowledge of the being who is the equivalent of *Bunjil* is almost entirely restricted to the initiated men. The old women know that there is a supernatural being in the sky, but only as *Mungan-ngaua*, 'our father.' It is only at the last and the most secret part of the ceremonies that the novices are made aware of the teachings as to *Mungan-ngaua*, and this is the only name for this being used by the Kurnai. . . .

The conception of *Baiame* may be seen from Ridley's statements, and so far as I now quote them, may be accepted as sufficiently accurate. I have omitted the colouring which appears to be derived from his mental bias as a missionary to blacks. He says that *Baiame* is the name in Kamilaroi of the maker (from *Biai*, 'to make or build') who created and preserves all things. Generally invisible, he has, they believe, appeared in human form, and has bestowed on their race various gifts.

The following is the statement of one of the early settlers in the Kamilaroi country, and, I think, gives the aboriginal idea of *Baiame* free from any tinge derived from our beliefs. If you ask a Kamilaroi man 'Who made that?' referring to something, he replies, 'Baiame deah,' that is 'Baiame, I suppose.' It is said that Baiame came from the westward long ago to Golarinbri on the Barwon, and stayed there four or five days, when he went away to the eastward with his two wives. They believe that some time he will return again. . . .

The belief in *Daramulun*, the 'father,' and *Biamban*, or 'master,' is common to all of the tribes who attend the *Yuin Kuringal*. I have described them at length in chapter IX, and may now summarize the teachings of the ceremonies. Long ago *Daramulun* lived on the earth with his mother *Ngalalbal*. Originally the earth was bare 'like the sky, as hard as a stone,' and the land extended far out where the sea is now. There were no men or women, but only animals, birds, and reptiles. He placed trees on the earth. After Kaboka, the thrush, had caused a great flood on the earth, which covered all the coast country, there were no people left, excepting some who crawled out of the water on to Mount Dromedary. Then *Daramulun* went up to the sky, where he lives and watches the actions of men. It was he who first made the *Kuringal* and the bull-roarer, the sound of which represents his voice. He told the Yuin what to do, and he gave them the laws which the old people have handed down from father to son to this time. He gives the *Gommeras* their power to use the *Joias*, and other magic. When a man dies and his *Tulugal* (spirit)

4

goes away, it is *Daramulun* who meets it and takes care of it. It is a man's shadow which goes up to *Daramulun*. . . .

It seems quite clear that *Nurrundere, Nurelli, Bunjil, Mungan-ngaua, Daramulun,* and *Baiame* all represent the same being under different names. To this may be reasonably added *Koin* of the Lake Macquarie tribes, *Maamba, Birral,* and *Kohin* of those on the Herbert River, thus extending the range of this belief certainly over the whole of Victoria and of New South Wales, up to the eastern boundaries of the tribes of the Darling River. If the Queensland coast tribes are included, then the western bounds might be indicated by a line drawn from the mouth of the Murray River to Cardwell, including the Great Dividing Range, with some of the fall inland in New South Wales. This would define the part of Australia in which a belief exists in an anthropomorphic supernatural being, who lives in the sky, and who is supposed to have some kind of influence on the morals of the natives. No such belief seems to obtain in the remainder of Australia, although there are indications of a belief in anthropomorphic beings inhabiting the sky-land. . . .

This supernatural being, by whatever name he is known, is represented as having at one time dwelt on the earth, but afterwards to have ascended to a land beyond the sky, where he still remains, observing mankind. As *Daramulun*, he is said to be able to 'go anywhere and do anything.' He can be invisible; but when he makes himself visible, it is in the form of an old man of the Australian race. He is evidently everlasting, for he existed from the beginning of all things, and he still lives. But in being so, he is merely in that state in which, these aborigines believe, every one would be if not prematurely killed by evil magic.

A. W. Howitt, *The Native Tribes of South-East Australia* (London, 1904), pp. 491-500

See also no. 142

AFRICAN HIGH GODS

Like many celestial Supreme Beings of 'primitive' peoples, the High Gods of a great number of African ethnic groups are regarded as creators, all-powerful, benevolent, and so forth; but they play a rather insignificant part in the religious life. Being either too distant or too good to need a real cult, they are invoked only in cases of great crisis. (Cf. M. Eliade, 'Patterns in Comparative Religion,' trans. Rosemary Sheed [New York: Sheed and Ward, 1958], pp. 47-50.)

2. NZAMBI, THE HIGH GOD OF THE BAKONGO

The Bakongo tribe is native to the lower Congo River area.

Nzambi Mpungu is a being, invisible, but very powerful, who has made all, men and things, even fetishes which he has given to men for their good. 'If he had not given us our fetishes, we should all be dead long ago.' He intervenes in the creation of every child, he punishes those who violate his prohibitions. They render him no worship, for he has need of none and is inaccessible. On earth man lives with his incessant needs to satisfy; the aged have there a privileged position. Above all is Nzambi, the sovereign Master, unapproachable, who has placed man here below to take him away some day, at the hour of death. He watches man, searches him out everywhere and takes him away, inexorably, young or old. . . . Among the laws there are nkondo mi Nzambi, 'God's prohibitions,' the violation of which constitutes a sumu ku Nzambi [a sin against Nzambi], and an ordinary sanction of this is lufwa lumbi 'a bad death.'

Van Wing, Études Bakongo (Brussels, 1921; pp. 170 ff.) as translated by Edwin W. Smith in Smith (ed.), African Ideas of God: A Symposium (2nd ed.; London, 1950), p. 159

3. THE SUPREME BEING OF THE ISOKO (SOUTHERN NIGERIA)

Isoko religion begins with Cghene the Supreme Being, who is believed to have created the world and all peoples, including the Isoko. He lives in the sky which is a part of him, sends rain and sunshine, and shows his anger through thunder. Cghene is entirely beyond human comprehension, has never been seen, is sexless, and is only known by his actions, which have led men to speak of Cghene as 'him,' because he is thought of as the creator and therefore father of all the Isokos. He is spoken of as Our Father never as My Father. Cghene always punishes evil and rewards good, a belief that leads the Isokos to blame witchcraft for any evil which may happen to a good man. As however Cghene is so distant and unknowable, he has no temples or priests, and no prayers or sacrifices are offered to him direct. To bridge the gulf between himself and man, Cghene appointed an intermediary, called *oyise*, which is referred to as *uko Cghene* or 'messenger of Cghene.' This *oyise* is a pole about eight feet long made from the *oyise* tree, erected after a seven-fold offering to Cghene, in the compound of the oldest member of the family, and only in his. Before this pole the family elder throws his used chewing stick each morning and offers prayer for the family and town. Through *oyise*, Cghene can be invoked in case of calamity or need.

James W. Telch, 'The Isoko Tribe,' *Africa*, VII (1934), pp. 160 73; quotation from p. 163

4. NGAI, THE HIGH GOD OF THE KIKUYU

The Kikuyu are a Bantu-speaking tribe of East Africa.

First we have Gothaithaya Ngai, which means 'to beseech Ngai,' or 'to worship Ngai.' Ngai is a name of the High God. The difference between deity worship and ancestor worship is demonstrated by the fact that Gothaithaya is never used in connection with ancestral spirits.

The Conception of a Deity. The Kikuyu believes in one God, Ngai, the Creator and giver of all things. He has no father, mother, or companion of any kind. He loves or hates people according to their behaviour. The Creator lives in the sky, but has temporary homes on earth, situated on mountains, where he may rest during his visits. The visits are made with a view to his carrying out a kind of 'general inspection,' *Koroora thi*, and to bring blessings and punishments to the people. . . . Ngai cannot be seen by mortal eyes. He is a distant being and takes but little interest in individuals in their daily walks of life. Yet at the crises of their lives he is called upon. At the birth, initiation, marriage and death of every Kikuyu, communication is established on his behalf with Ngai. The ceremonies for these four events leave no doubt as to the importance of the spiritual assistance which is essential to them. . . . In the ordinary way of everyday life, there are no prayers or religious ceremonies, such as 'morning and evening prayers.' So long as people and things go well and prosper, it is taken for granted that God is pleased with the general behaviour of the people and the welfare of the country. In this happy state there is no need for prayers. Indeed they are inadvisable, for Ngai must not needlessly be bothered. It is only when humans are in real need that they must approach him without fear of disturbing him and incurring his wrath. But when people meet to discuss public affairs or decide a case, or at public dances, they offer prayers for protection and guidance. When a man is stricken by lightning it is said: 'He has been smashed to smithereens for seeing Ngai in the act of cracking his joints in readiness to go to smash and chase away his enemies.'

It is said that lightning is a visible representation of some of God's weapons which he uses on ahead to warn people of his coming and to prepare and clear the way. His approach is foretold only by the sounds of his own preparations. Thunder is the cracking of his joints, as a warrior limbering up for action.

Jomo Kenyatta, 'Kikuyu Religion, Ancestor-Worship, and Sacrificial Practices,' *Africa*, x (1937), pp. 308-28; quotation from pp. 308-9

5. LEZA, THE HIGH GOD OF THE BA-ILA OF NORTHERN RHODESIA

Long ago the Ba-ila did not know Leza as regards his affairs—no, all that they knew about him, was that he created us, and also his unweariedness in doing things. As at present when the rainy season is annoying and he does not fall, when then they ask of Leza different things: they say now: 'Leza annoys by not falling': then later when he falls heavily they say: 'Leza falls too much.' If there is cold they say 'Leza makes it cold,' and if it is not they say, 'Leza is much too hot, let it be overclouded.' All the same, Leza as he is the Compassionate, that is to say, as he is Merciful, he does not get angry, he doesn't give up falling, he doesn't give up doing them all good—no, whether they curse, whether they mock him, whether they grumble at him, he does good to all at all times, that is how they trust him always. But as for

8

seeing always his affairs, no, the Ba-ila do not know, all they say is: Leza is the good-natured one; he is one from whom you beg different things. We Ba-ila have no more that we know.

Edwin W. Smith and A. M. Dale, *The Ila-speaking People of Northern Rhodesia*, II (London, 1920), p. 199

6. THE SUPREME BEING OF THE HERERO

The Herero are a Bantu tribe of South-West Africa.

'The Hereros know a supreme being whom they call by two names: Ndjambi Karunga. The name Karunga has an Ovambo derivation and is only known intimately to those Hereros, who have been in contact with the Ovambo in former times. . . . Ndjambi is the Heavenly God. He lives in Heaven, yet is omnipresent. His most striking characteristic is kindness. Human life is due to and dependent on him and all blessings ultimately come from him. He who dies a natural death is carried away by Ndjambi. As his essence is kindness people cherish no fear but a veneration for him. As his blessings are the gifts of his kindness without any moral claims, the belief in Ndjambi has no moral strength, nor has the worship of Ndjambi become a cult. At best his name is invoked only in thanksgiving after some unexpected luck or they pray to him when all other means of help fail. For the rest, the utterance of his name is not allowed. In reply to a question I put to a Tjimba woman in the Kaokoveld as to the abode of Ndjambi Karunga, she said: 'He stays in the clouds because, when the clouds rise, his voice is clearly heard,' and further research has brought to light that the Tjimba look upon Ndjambi as the giver of rain.' (H. Vedder, *The Native Tribes of South-West Africa*, Capetown, 1928, p. 164.)

Dr. Vedder's statement that the sacred name should not be uttered is significant. It explains partly, if not wholly, why the missionaries who had lived in close contact with the Herero since 1844 heard his name for the first time only in 1871.

Dr. H. Vedder, as quoted and commented on by Edwin W. Smith (ed.), *African Ideas of God: A Symposium* (2nd ed.; London, 1950), pp. 132-3

7. RALUVHIMBA, THE HIGH GOD OF THE VENDA

The Venda are a Bantu tribe of the northern Transvaal.

The name is composed of the prefix *Ra-*, which is honorific and perhaps connected with the idea of 'Father'; *luvhimba* is the eagle, the bird that soars aloft. It symbolizes the great power which travels through the cosmos, using the heavenly phenomena as its instruments.

'Raluvhimba is connected with the beginning of the world and is supposed to live somewhere in the heavens and to be connected with all astronomical and physical phenomena. . . . A shooting star is Raluvhimba travelling; his voice is heard in the thunder; comets, lightning, meteors, earthquakes, prolonged drought, floods, pests, and epidemics—in fact, all the natural phenomena which affect the people as a whole—are revelations of the great god. In thunderstorms he appears as a great fire near the chief's kraal, whence he booms his desires to the chief in a voice of thunder; this fire always disappears before any person can reach it. At these visitations the chief enters his hut and, addressing Raluvhimba as *Makhulu* [Grandfather], converses with him, the voice of the god replying either from the thatch of the hut or from a tree nearby; Raluvhimba then passes on in a further clap of thunder. Occasionally he is angry with the chief and takes revenge on the people by sending them a drought or a flood, or possibly by opening an enormous cage in the heavens and letting loose a swarm of locusts on the land.'

(H. A. Stayt, *The Bavenda*, Oxford, 1931, p. 236)

Raluvhimba, it is said, was wont to manifest himself by appearing from time to time as a great flame on a platform of rock above a certain cave. With the flame there came a sound as of clanking irons, on hearing which the people shouted with joy and their cries passed on throughout the country. The Chief mounted to the platform where he called upon Raluvhimba, thanked him for revealing himself and prayed on behalf of his people for rain, felicity and peace.

He is at times greeted spontaneously by the whole people in a way that is most unusual among the southern Bantu. The Rev. G. Westphal of the Berlin Mission relates that in 1917 a meteor burst in the middle of the day making a strange humming sound followed by a thunder-like crash. This portent was greeted by the people, not with terror but with cries of joy. Another missionary, the Rev. McDonald, tells how after a slight tremor of the earth there was an extraordinary clamour among the people, the lululuing of women, clapping of hands and shouting. 'The whole tribe was greeting Raluvhimba who was passing through the country.' People say that during an earthquake they hear a noise in the sky similar to thunder. Then they clap their hands to welcome the mysterious god and pray: 'Give us rain! Give us health!'

Dr. H. A. Junod says that Raluvhimba is regarded as the maker and former of everything and as the rain-giver. If rain is scarce and starvation threatens, people complain: 'Raluvhimba wants to destroy us.' They say the same if floods spoil their fields. Prayers and sacrifices are offered in times of drought. There is some notion of Raluvhimba as Providence. He takes care not only of the tribe as a whole but of individual members. When a man has narrowly escaped drowning he will say: 'I have been saved by Raluvhimba, Mudzimu.'

Raluvhimba is identified with Mwari (or Nwali) whose earthly abode (like Yahwe's on Mount Sinai) is in the Matopo Hills of Southern Rhodesia. Every year the Venda used to send a special messenger (whose office was hereditary) with a black ox and a piece of black cloth as an offering to Mwari. The black ox was set free in a forest to join the god's large herd which had accumulated there.

Edwin W. Smith, 'The Idea of God among South African Tribes' in Smith (ed.), *African Ideas of God: A Symposium* (2nd ed.; London, 1950), pp. 124-6

See also nos. 51, 67, 91, 126, 127, 299

NORTH AMERICAN INDIANS

8. WAKAN TANKA, THE SUPREME DEITY OF THE DAKOTA

Following are the words of Sword, an Oglala of the Teton division of the Dakota Indians, as recorded by J. R. Walker.

Every object in the world has a spirit and that spirit is *wakan*. Thus the spirits of the tree or things of that kind, while not like the spirit of man, are also *wakan*. *Wakan* comes from the *wakan* beings. These wakan beings are greater than mankind in the same way that mankind is greater than animals. They are never born and never die. They can do many things that mankind cannot do. Mankind can pray to the wakan beings for help. There are many of these beings but all are of four kinds. The word *Wakan Tanka* means all of the *wakan* beings because they are all as if one. *Wakan Tanka Kin* signifies the chief or leading *Wakan* being which is the Sun. However, the most powerful of the *Wakan* beings is *Nagi Tanka*, the Great Spirit who is also *Taku Skanskan*. *Taku Skanskan* signifies the Blue, in other words, the Sky. . . . Mankind is permitted to pray to the *Wakan* beings. If their prayer is directed to all the good *Wakan* beings, they should pray to *Wakan Tanka*; but if the prayer is offered to only one of these beings, then the one addressed should be named. . . . *Wakan Tanka* is like sixteen different persons; but each person is *kan*. Therefore, they are only the same as one.

J. R. Walker, *The Sun Dance and Other Ceremonies of the Oglala Division of the Teton Dakota* (American Museum of Natural History, Anthropological Papers, vol. XVI, part II (1917), pp. 152-3)

9. THE 'GREAT SPIRIT' OF THE LENAPE

The Lenape (or Delaware) Indians, an important Algonquian tribe, occupied a large area from Ontario southward into the middle Atlantic region, and westward principally in Oklahoma.

All the Lenape so far questioned, whether followers of the native or of the Christian religion, unite in saying that their people have always believed in a chief *Mani 'to*, a leader of all the gods, in short, in a Great Spirit or Supreme Being, the other *mani 'towuk* for the greater part being merely agents appointed by him. His name, according to present Unami usage is *Gicelĕmû 'kaong*, usually translated 'great spirit,' but meaning literally, 'creator.' Directly, or through the *mani- 'towuk* his agents, he created the earth and eveything in it, and gave to the Lenape all they possessed, 'the trees, the waters, the fire that springs from flint,—everything.' To him the people pray in their greatest ceremonies, and give thanks for the benefits he has given them. Most of their direct worship, however, is addressed to the *mani 'towuk* his agents, to whom he has given charge of the elements, and with whom the people feel they have a closer personal relation, as their actions are seen in every sunrise and thunderstorm, and felt in every wind that blows across woodland and prairie. Moreover, as the Creator lives in the twelfth or highest heaven above the earth, it takes twelve shouts or cries to reach his ear.

M. R. Harrington, *Religion and Ceremonies of the Lenape* (New York, 1921), pp. 18-19

10. TIRAWA, THE SUPREME GOD OF THE PAWNEE

Once among the strongest tribes of the Plains Indians, the Pawnee were found from the shores of the Platte River in Nebraska south to the Arkansas River. Today they live mostly in Oklahoma.

'The white man,' said the Kurahus, 'speaks of a heavenly Father; we say Tirawa atius, the Father above, but we do not think of Tirawa as a person. We think of Tirawa as in everything, as the Power which has arranged and thrown down from above everything that man needs. What the Power above, Tirawa atius, is like, no one knows; no one has been there.'

When Kawas explains to the Kurahus the meaning of the signs in the East, 'she tells him that Tirawa atius there moves upon Darkness, the Night, and causes her to bring forth the Dawn. It is the breath of the new-born Dawn, the child of Night and Tirawa atius, which is felt by all the powers and all things above and below and which gives them new life for the new day. . . .'

H. B. Alexander, *The World's Rim* (Lincoln, Neb.: University of Nebraska Press, 1953), p. 132; quoting and summarizing Alice C. Fletcher, *The Hako: A Pawnee Ceremony* (Bureau of American Ethnology, Twenty-second Annual Report, part 2, 1904)

See also nos. 44, 45

POLYNESIA, COLOMBIA, LABRADOR, NEW GUINEA

11. THE MAORI SUPREME BEING (POLYNESIA)

The core of the esoteric theology of the Maori was the concept of the Supreme Io which remained wholly unrevealed to foreign enquirers for many decades after the first contact of Europeans and Maori. I cannot help feeling that our lack of knowledge of such a supreme god in other island groups is due largely to the fact that the knowledge was limited to the ancient priesthood, whose rules would have compelled them to conceal from outsiders the most sacred of the lore; while personal instinct would at the same time have led them to shelter their hallowed belief from strangers with the attitude typical of practically all the early enquirers. With the ancient priesthoods, the knowledge of the great body of the most sacred Polynesian lore died. The following pictures well the attitude of Maori priests towards the indiscreetly inquisitive and disrespectful. Tregear writes:

'C. O. Davis mentions that when attempting to question an old priest on the subject of the ancient Maori worship of the Supreme Being he was refused information, and politely referred to another priest 100 miles away. Probably that priest would have referred him again to someone else and so on. Each initiate into the sacred mysteries considered his knowledge as a trust to be guarded against the outer world, and it is only under most exceptional circumstances that information could be acquired. Some gods could only be named in the Whare Kura and Wharewanagna (temples) of the tribe. To utter "the ineffable name" (Io) under a roof of any kind was to blaspheme most frightfully, and would be a sacrilege that only an ignorant person (religiously ignorant) like a European would have the depravity to attempt. Even the names of ancestors, as god-descended, would not be regarded as treated with due respect if mentioned at certain times or in unsuitable localities. A European student of Maori lore once ventured to speak to an old priest whom he met in a country store (shop) and asked him some question about ancient history. The Maori turned round with a disgusted look and remarked, "This is no place in which to speak of solemn things,". . . Only one who loved the

14

enquirer and dared unknown terrors for the sake of that love would answer such questions (about sacred things) or repeat the consecrated hymns for him. It is not unusual for a priest after going a certain length to say, "If I tell you any more death will overtake me," or "I must not repeat what follows, because there is now no priest alive sacred enough to perform the ceremonies necessary to purify me from such sacrilege." Another has been known to say, "The presence of the Christian God has silenced the Maori gods, but the gods of the Maori still hold us in their power, and if I break their laws they will punish me with death."'

The mere fact of the existence of Io was unknown to most Maoris. Best writes that:

"The number of men initiated into the cult of Io was but small; only members of the higher grade of priestly experts and men of high-class families, were allowed to learn the ritual pertaining to it. The common folk apparently had no part in it and it is doubtful if they were even allowed to know the name of the Supreme Being. This cult of Io was an esoteric one; that of the lower tribal gods may be termed exoteric. All ritual and ceremonial pertaining to Io was retained in the hands of the superior priesthood, by no means a numerous body. It may be described as an aristocratic cultus, known only to such experts and the more important chiefs. It is quite probable, indeed, that this superior creed may have been too exalted for ordinary minds, that such would prefer to depend on more accessible and less moral deities.

'It is interesting to note that no form of offering or sacrifice was made to Io, that no image of him was ever made, and that he had no *aria*, or form of incarnation, such as inferior gods had.'

E. S. Craighill Handy, *Polynesian Religion*, Bernice P. Bishop Museum Bulletin 34 (Honolulu, 1927), pp. 95-6; quoting Edward Tregear, *The Maori Race* (Wanganui, 1904), pp. 450-2, and Elsdon Best, *Some Aspects of Maori Myth and Religion* (Dominion Museum Monograph no. 1, Wellington, 1922), p. 20

See also no. 47

12. THE UNIVERSAL MOTHER AND SUPREME DEITY

The following comes from the Kagaba people of Colombia in South America.

'The mother of our songs, the mother of all our seed, bore us in the the beginning of things and so she is the mother of all types of men, the mother of all nations. She is the mother of the thunder, the mother of the streams, the mother of trees and of all things. She is the mother of the world and of the older brothers, the stone-people. She is the mother of the fruits of the earth and of all things. She is the mother of our youngest brothers, the French and the strangers. She is the mother of our dance paraphernalia, of all our temples and she is the only mother we possess. She alone is the mother of the fire and the Sun and the Milky Way. . . . She is the mother of the rain and the only mother we possess. And she has left us a token in all the temples . . . a token in the form of songs and dances.'

   She has no cult, and no prayers are really directed to her, but when the fields are sown and the priests chant their incantations the Kagaba say, 'And then we think of the one and only mother of the growing things, of the mother of all things.' One prayer was recorded. 'Our mother of the growing fields, our mother of the streams, will have pity upon us. For whom do we belong? Whose seeds are we? To our mother alone do we belong.'

Paul Radin, *Monotheism among Primitive Peoples*
New York, p. 15; translating and quoting K. T.
Preuss

13. A SOUTH AMERICAN EPIPHANY OF THE SUN GOD

The Apinayé, one of the Gé tribes of eastern Brazilia, regard the Sun as creator and father of men. They address the Sun God as 'my father' and he calls men his children. The following experience was told to the anthropologist Curt Nimuendaju by an Apinayé village chief.

'I was hunting near the sources of the Botica creek. All along the journey there I had been agitated and was constantly startled without knowing why.

'Suddenly I saw him standing under the drooping branches of a big steppe tree. He was standing there erect. His club was braced against the ground beside him, his hand he held on the hilt. He was tall and light-skinned, and his hair nearly descended to the ground behind him. His whole body was painted, and on the outer side of his legs were broad red stripes. His eyes were exactly like two stars. He was very handsome.

'I recognized at once that it was he. Then I lost all courage. My hair stood on end, and my knees were trembling. I put my gun aside, for I thought to myself that I should have to address him, but I could not utter a sound because he was looking at me unwaveringly. Then I lowered my head in order to get hold of myself and stood thus for a long time. When I had grown somewhat calmer, I raised my head. He was still standing and looking at me. Then I pulled myself together and walked several steps toward him, then I could not go any further for my knees gave way. I again remained standing for a long time, then lowered my head, and tried again to regain composure. When I raised my eyes again, he had already turned away and was slowly walking through the steppe.

'Then I grew very sad. I kept standing there for a long time after he had vanished, then I walked under the tree where he had stood. I saw his footprints, painted red with urucú at the edges; beside them was the print of his clubhead. I picked up my gun and returned to the village. On the way I managed to kill two deer, which approached me without the least shyness. At home I told my father everything. Then all scolded me for not having had the courage to talk to him.

'At night while I was asleep he reappeared to me. I addressed him, and he said he had been waiting for me in the steppe to talk to me, but since I had not approached he had gone away. He led me some distance behind the house and there showed me a spot on the ground where, he said, something was lying in storage for me. Then he vanished.

'The next morning I immediately went there and touched the ground with the tip of my foot, perceiving something hard buried there. But others came to call me to go hunting. I was ashamed to stay behind and joined them. When we returned, I at once went back to the site he had shown me, but did not find anything any more.

'Today I know that I was very stupid then. I should certainly have received from him great self-assurance (segurança) if I had been able to talk to him. But I was still very young then; today I should act quite differently.'

Curt Nimuendaju, *The Apinayé* (Washington, D.C., 1939), 136-7

14. THE MASTER OF THE CARIBOU

A belief of the Naskapi Indians of the Labrador Peninsula.

In the interior between Ungava Bay and Hudson's Bay is a distant country where no Indians will go under any consideration for the following reason. There is a range of big mountains pure white in colour formed neither of snow, ice, nor white rock, but of caribou hair. They are shaped like a house and so they are known as Caribou House. One man of the Petisigabau band says there are two houses. In this enormous cavity live thousands upon thousands of caribou under the overlordship of a human being who is white and dressed in black. Some say there are several of them and they have beards. He is master of the caribou and will not permit anyone to come within some one hundred and fifty miles of his abode, the punishment being death. Within his realm the various animals are two or three times their ordinary size. The few Indians who have approached the region say that the caribou enter and leave their kingdom each year, passing through a valley between two high mountains about fifteen miles apart. And it is also asserted that the deer hair on the ground here is several feet in depth, that for miles around the cast-off antlers on the ground form a layer waist deep, that the caribou paths leading back and forth there are so deep as to reach a man's waist, and that a young caribou going along in one would be visible only by its head.

F. G. Speck, *Naskapi, The Savage Hunters of the Labrador Peninsula* (Norman, Okla.: University of Oklahoma Press, 1935), p. 84

15. HAINUWELE AND THE 'CREATIVE MURDER' (CERAM, NEW GUINEA)

The Marind-anim apply the term *dema* to the divine creators and primordial beings who existed in mythical times. The *dema* are described sometimes in human form, sometimes in the form of animals and plants. The central myth narrates the slaying of the *dema*-divinity by the *dema*-men of the primordial time. Especially famous is the myth of the girl Hainuwele, recorded by A. E. Jensen in Ceram, one of the islands of the New Guinea Archipelago. In substance it runs:

In mythical Times, a man named Ameta, out hunting, came on a wild boar. Trying to escape, the boar was drowned in a lake. On its tusk Ameta found a coconut. That night he dreamed of the coconut and was commanded to plant it, which he did the next morning. In three days a coconut palm sprang up, and three days later it flowered. Ameta climbed it to cut some flowers and make a drink from them. But he cut his finger and the blood dropped on a flower. Nine days later he found a girl-child on the flower. Ameta took her and wrapped her in coconut fronds. In three days the child became a marriageable girl, and he named her Hainuwele ('coconut branch'). During the great Maro festival Hainuwele stood in the middle of the dancing place and for nine nights distributed gifts to the dancers. But on the ninth day the men dug a grave in the middle of the dancing place and threw Hainuwele into it during the dance. The grave was filled in and men danced on it.

The next morning, seeing that Hainuwele did not come home, Ameta divined that she had been murdered. He found the body, disinterred it, and cut it into pieces, which he buried in various places, except the arms. The buried pieces gave birth to plants previously unknown, especially to tubers, which since then are the chief food of human beings. Ameta took Hainuwele's arms to another *dema*-divinity, Satene. Satene drew a spiral with nine turns on a dancing ground and placed herself at the centre of it. From Hainuwele's arms she made a door, and summoned the dancers. 'Since you have killed,' she said, 'I will no longer live here. I shall leave this very day. Now you will have to come to me through this door.' Those who were able to pass through it remained human beings. The others were changed into animals (pigs, birds, fish) or spirits. Satene announced that after her going men would meet her only after their death, and she vanished from the surface of the Earth.

A. E. Jensen has shown the importance of this myth for an understanding of the religion and world image of the paleocultivators. The murder of a *dema* divinity by the *dema*, the ancestors of present humanity, ends an epoch (which cannot be considered 'paradisal') and opens that in which we live today. The *dema* became men, that is, sexed and mortal beings. As for the murdered *dema*-divinity, she survives both in her own 'creations' (food, plants, animals, etc.) and in the house of the dead into which she was changed, or in the 'mode of being of death,' which she established by her own demise.

M. Eliade, *Myth and Reality* (New York, 1963), pp. 104-5; translated and abridged from A. E. Jensen, *Das religiöse Weltbild einer frühen Kultur* (Stuttgart, 1948), pp. 35-8

B. GODS OF THE ANCIENT NEAR EAST, ANCIENT INDIA, AND JAPAN

16. ENKI, A SUMERIAN HIGH GOD

'Enki and the World Order' is one of the longest and best preserved of the extant Sumerian narrative poems. The poem begins with a hymn of praise addressed to Enki; some of it is destroyed and unintelligible, but generally speaking, it seems to exalt Enki as the god who watches over the universe and is responsible for the fertility of field and farm, flock and herd. It continues to follow the same motif at some length, with Enki now praising himself, now being praised by the gods. Next, a badly damaged passage seems to describe the various rites and rituals performed by some of the more important priests and spiritual leaders of Sumer in Enki's Abzu-shrine. The scene shifts again to reveal Enki in his boat, passing from city to city to 'decree the fates' and render proper exaltation to each. Two inimical lands are not so fortunate; he destroys them and carries off their wealth.

Enki now turns from the fates of the various lands which made up the Sumerian inhabited world and performs a whole series of acts vital to the earth's fertility and productiveness. He fills the Tigris with life-giving water, then appoints the god Enbilulu, the 'canal inspector,' to make sure that the Tigris and Euphrates function properly. He 'calls' the marshland and the canebrake, supplies them with fish and reeds, and again appoints a deity for them. He erects his own shrine by the sea and places the goddess Nanshe in charge of it. Similarly, he 'calls' the earth's plow, yoke, and furrow, the cultivated field, the pickaxe, and brick mould; he turns to the high plain, covers it with vegetation and cattle, stall and sheepfolds; he fixes the borders and cities and states; finally he attends to 'woman's task,' particularly the weaving of cloth. For each realm a deity is appointed.

The poem comes to an end in yet another key as the ambitious and aggressive Inanna complains that she has been slighted and left without any special powers and perogatives. Enki reassures her with a recitation of her own insignia and provinces.

Enki, the king of the Abzu, overpowering in his majesty, speaks up with authority:

'My father, the king of the universe,
Brought me into existence in the universe,
My ancestor, the king of all the lands,
Gathered together all the me's, placed the me's in my hand.
From the Ekur, the house of Enlil,
I brought craftsmanship to my Abzu of Eridu.
I am the fecund seed, engendered by the great wild ox, I am the first born son of An,
I am the "great storm" who goes forth out of the "great below," I am the lord of the Land,
I am the gugal of the chieftains, I am the father of all the lands,
I am the "big brother" of the gods, I am he who brings full prosperity,
I am the record keeper of heaven and earth,
I am the ear and the mind of all the lands,
I am he who directs justice with the king An on An's dais,
I am he who decrees the fates with Enlil in the "mountain of wisdom,"
He placed in my hand the decreeing of the fates of the "place where the sun rises,"
I am he to whom Nintu pays due homage,
I am he who has been called a good name by Ninhursag,
I am the leader of the Anunnaki,
I am he who has been born as the first son of the holy An.'

After the lord had uttered (his) exaltedness,
After the great prince had himself pronounced his praise,
The Anunnaki came before him in prayer and supplication:
'Lord who directs craftsmanship,
Who makes decisions, the glorified; Enki, praise!'

For a second time, because of his great joy,
Enki, the king of the Abzu, in his majesty, speaks up with authority:
'I am the lord, I am one whose command is unquestioned, I am the foremost in all things,
At my command the stalls have been built, the sheepfolds have been enclosed,
When I approached heaven a rain of prosperity poured down from heaven,
When I approached the earth, there was a high flood,
When I approached its green meadows,
The heaps and mounds were piled up at my word.

....

[After the almost unintelligible description of Enki's rites, Enki proceeds to decree the fates of a number of cities. Ur is one example.]

He proceeded to the shrine Ur,
Enki, the king of the Abzu decrees its fate:
'City possessing all that is appropriate, water-washed, firm-standing ox,
Dais of abundance of the highland, knees open, green like a mountain,
Hashur-grove, wide of shade—he who is lordly because of his might
Has directed your perfect me's,
Enlil, the "great mountain," has pronounced your lofty name in the
    universe.
City whose fate has been decreed by Enlil,
Shrine Ur, may you rise heaven high.'

....

[Enki next stocks the land with various items of prosperity: A deity is placed in charge of each. For example:]

He directed the plow and the . . . yoke,
The great prince Enki put the 'horned oxen' in the . . .
Opened the holy furrows,
Made grow the grain in the cultivated field.
The lord who dons the diadem, the ornament of the high plain,
The robust, the farmer of Enlil,
Enkimdu, the man of the ditch and dike,
Enki placed in charge of them.

The lord called the cultivated field, put there the checkered grain,
Heaped up its . . . grain, the checkered grain, the innuba-grain into
    piles,
Enki multiplied the heaps and mounds,
With Enlil he spread wide the abundance in the Land,
Her whose head and side are dappled, whose face is honey-covered,
The Lady, the procreatress, the vigour of the Land, the 'life' of the
    black-heads,
Ashnan, the nourishing bread, the bread of all,
Enki placed in charge of them.

....

He built stalls, directed the purification rites,
Erected sheepfolds, put there the best fat and milk,
Brought joy to the dining halls of the gods,

23

In the vegetation-like plain he made prosperity prevail.

....

He filled the Ekur, the house of Enlil, with possessions,
Enlil rejoiced with Enki, Nippur was joyous,
He fixed the borders, demarcated them with boundary stones,
Enki, for the Anunnaki,
Erected dwelling places in the cities,
Set up fields for them in the countryside,
The hero, the bull who comes forth out of the hashur (forest), who
*   roars lion-like,*
The valiant Utu, the bull who stands secure, who proudly displays
*   his power,*
The father of the great city, the place where the sun rises, the great
*   herald of holy An,*
The judge, the decision-maker of the gods,
Who wears a lapis lazuli beard, who comes forth from the holy heaven,
*   the . . . heaven,*
Utu, the son born of Ningal,
Enki placed in charge of the entire universe.

[The remainder of the extant text is devoted to Inanna's challenge
and Enki's response.]

> Translation by Samuel Noah Kramer, in his *The
> Sumerians. Their History, Culture and Character*
> (Chicago: University of Chicago Press, 1963), pp. 174-
> 83; introductory material paraphrased and summarized
> by M. Eliade from Kramer, *op. cit.*, pp. 171-4

See also no. 133

17. THE EGYPTIAN HIGH GOD IN THE AGE OF THE COFFIN TEXTS

('Coffin Texts,' 714)

The so-called 'Coffin Texts,' inscribed on the interior of coffins, belong
to the Middle Kingdom (2250-1580 B.C.).

I was [the spirit in ?] the Primeval Waters,
he who had no companion when my name came into existence.
The most ancient form in which I came into existence was as a drowned
*   one.*

I was [also] he who came into existence as a circle,
he who was the dweller in his egg.
I was the one who began [everything], the dweller in the Primeval
  Waters.
First Hahu[1] emerged for me
and then I began to move.
I created my limbs in my 'glory.'
I was the maker of myself, in that I formed myself according to my
  desire and in accord with my heart.

Note

1 Hahu, the wind which began the separation of the waters and raised the sky.

Translated by R. T. Rundle Clark, in his *Myth and*
Symbol in Ancient Egypt (London, 1959), p. 74

18. ATUM, A BISEXUAL HIGH GOD

('Coffin Texts,' I, 161 ff.)

I am Atum, the creator of the Eldest Gods,
I am he who gave birth to Shu,
I am that great He-She,
I am he who did what seemed good to him,
I took my space in the place of my will,
Mine is the space of those who move along
like those two serpentine circles.

Translated by R. T. Rundle Clark, in his *Myth and*
Symbol in Ancient Egypt (London, 1959), p. 80

19. DEBATE BETWEEN OSIRIS AND THE HIGH GOD

('Book of the Dead,' Chapter 175)

After his death Osiris finds himself in a cheerless underworld and laments his lot.

OSIRIS O Atum! What is this desert place into which I have come?
  It has no water, it has no air,

25

    it is depth unfathomable, it is black as the blackest night.
I wander helplessly herein.
One cannot live here in peace of heart, nor may the longings
    of love be satisfied herein.

ATUM *You may live in peace of heart, I have provided illumination*
    in place of water and air, and satisfaction and quiet in the
    place of bread and beer. Thus spoke Atum.

OSIRIS *But shall I behold your face?*

ATUM *I will not allow you to suffer sorrow.*

OSIRIS *But every other god has his place in the Boat of Millions of*
    Years.

ATUM *Your place now belongs to your son Horus. Thus spoke Atum.*

OSIRIS *But will he be allowed to dispatch the Great Ones?*

ATUM *I have allowed him to dispatch the Great Ones, for he will*
    inherit your throne on the Isle of Fire.

OSIRIS *How good would it be if one god could see another!*

ATUM *My face will look upon your face.*

OSIRIS *But how long shall I live? says Osiris.*

ATUM *You will live more than millions of years, an era of millions,*
    but in the end I will destroy everything that I have created,
    the earth will become again part of the Primeval Ocean,
    like the Abyss of waters in their original state.
    Then I will be what will remain, just I and Osiris,
    when I will have changed myself back into the Old Serpent
    who knew no man and saw no god.

    How fair is that which I have done for Osiris, a fate different
    from that of all the other gods!
    I have given him the region of the dead while I have put his
    son Horus as heir upon his throne in the Isle of Fire;
    I have thus made his place for him in the Boat of Millions of
    Years, in that Horus remains on his throne to carry on his
    work.

OSIRIS *But will not also the soul of Seth be sent to the West—a fate*
    different from that of all other gods?

ATUM *I shall hold his soul captive in the Boat of the Sun—such is*
    my will—
    so that he will no longer terrorize the Divine Company.

Translation and introductory note by R. T. Rundle
Clark, in his *Myth and Symbol in Ancient Egypt*
(London, 1959), pp. 139-40

20. AMENHOTEP IV AND THE HYMN TO ATEN

At the time when Egypt was at the height of her career as a world power during the New Kingdom, the land was shaken by a revolutionary religious doctrine which threatened to sweep away the theological dogmas of centuries. The key figure in this iconoclastic movement was the Pharaoh Amenhotep IV who came to the throne *c.* 1370 B.C. to reign as co-regent with his father Amenhotep III (*c.* 1397-1360 B.C.). This youth, frail of body, with the temperament of a dreamer and the fanatical zeal of a reformer, inspired the somewhat extravagant description of him as 'the first individual in human history' (J. H. Breasted). So romantic a figure has he appeared to historians, that many have credited him with originating the worship of the god Aten and establishing the first monotheistic faith.

There is, however, a continually increasing body of evidence which points to the fact that the cult of Aten had developed before the time of Amenhotep IV, indeed probably as early as the reign of Thutmose IV (*c.* 1411-1397 B.C.). It is likely that the worship of Aten developed from the ancient cult of the Heliopolitan sun-god Re. In the course of time the syncretistic character of Egyptian religious thinking had led to the fusion of the god Re with many other deities such as Atum, Horus, and Amun, with the consequent assimilation of their characteristics and functions. The new cult paid homage to the physical orb of the sun (for which the Egyptian word was *aten*), stripped of its mythological accretions. Hence, except in the earliest period, no images or other representations of Aten were employed other than the figure of the sun disc with its rays extending towards the earth, each ending with a hand beneficently proffering the hieroglyphic symbol for life. . . . Central to the new faith was the idea of 'living on *ma 'at.*' This important term *ma 'at*, variously translated 'righteousness,' 'justice,' or 'truth,' meant basically the divinely ordained cosmic order. By the Middle Kingdom it had acquired the overtones of social justice. But Akhenaten's use of it emphasized the aspect of truth, by which he meant the subjective truth of the senses rather than the traditional objective, universal truth. This is consonant with the further observation that the Atenist faith was an intellectual rather than an ethical one, a fact which is apparent in the Aten Hymn. . . .

Noble though this doctrine may have been in many ways, it failed to win the approval or support of any but Akhenaten's circle of courtiers and adherents. To the people, as from time immemorial in

Egypt, the Pharaoh was himself a god, and Akhenaten did not seek to alter this. Only he and his family were privileged to offer worship directly to Aten; the people directed their prayers to the king, and through him the blessings of Aten were vouchsafed to them. It was inevitable that a doctrine of so contemplative and intellectual a nature would be incomprehensible to the common folk who either ignored it or adopted a hostile attitude towards it. This fact, combined with the lack of a spirit of compromise, so essential to the syncretistical-minded Egyptian, spelled disaster for Atenism. Under Akhenaten's co-regent and successor Smenkhkare, perhaps even before the former's death, a movement for reconciliation with the Amon-Re cult began. Before many years had passed, Atenism was forgotten, and the heretic King Akhenaten was anathematized by later generations. . . .

The first strophe extols the splendour of Aten as he rises in the heaven. Re, the sun-god of Heliopolis, is identified with Aten in line 7, . . . The next two strophes describe the terrors of darkness, when Aten is absent from the sky, as contrasted with the joys of day, when he has returned to pour his beneficent rays on the earth. . . . The fourth strophe speaks of Aten's life-giving powers in the world of nature. . . . The fifth and sixth strophes laud Aten as creator of the Universe. . . . In the seventh strophe Aten is hailed as a universal god, creating and sustaining all people. . . . The eighth strophe tells of Aten's concern for foreign lands. . . . Aten is viewed as the creator of the seasons in the next strophe.

1. *Thou dost appear beautiful on the horizon of heaven,*
     O living Aten, thou who wast the first to live.
   When thou hast risen on the eastern horizon,
     Thou hast filled every land with thy beauty.
5. *Thou art fair, great, dazzling, high above every land;*
     Thy rays encompass the lands to the very limit of all thou
       hast made.
   Being Re, thou dost reach to their limit
     And curb them [for] thy beloved son;
   Though thou art distant, they rays are upon the earth;
10. *Thou art in their faces, yet thy movements are unknown(?).*

   When thou dost set on the western horizon,
     The earth is in darkness, resembling death.
   Men sleep in the bed-chamber with their heads covered,
     Nor does one eye behold the other.
15. *Were all their goods stolen which are beneath their heads,*

They would not be aware of it.
Every lion has come forth from his den,
    All the snakes bite.
Darkness prevails, and the earth is in silence,
20.   Since he who made them is resting in his horizon.

At daybreak, when thou dost rise on the horizon,
    Dost shine as Aten by day,
Thou dost dispel the darkness
    And shed thy rays.
25. The two Lands are in a festive mood,
    Awake, and standing on (their) feet,
For thou hast raised them up;
    They cleanse their bodies and take (their) garments;
Their arms are (lifted) in adoration at thine appearing;
30.   The whole land performs its labour.

All beasts are satisfied with their pasture;
    Trees and plants are verdant.
The birds which fly from their nests, their wings are (spread)
    in adoration to thy soul;
All flocks skip with (their) feet;
35. All that fly up and alight
    Live when thou has risen [for] them.
Ships sail upstream and downstream alike,
    For every route is open at thine appearing.
The fish in the river leap before thee,
40.   For thy rays are in the midst of the sea.

Thou creator of issue in woman, who makest semen into mankind,
    And dost sustain the son in mother's womb,
Who dost soothe him with that which stills his tears,
    Thou nurse in the very womb, giving breath to sustain all
        thou dost make!
45. When he issues from the womb to breathe on the day of his birth,
    Thou dost open his mouth completely and supply his needs.
When the chick in the egg cheeps inside the shell,
    Thou givest it breath within it to sustain it.
Thou hast set it its appointed time in the egg to break it,
50.   That it may emerge from the egg to cheep at its appointed time;
    That it may walk with its feet when it emerges from it.

How manifold is that which thou hast made, hidden from view!

Thou sole god, there is no other like thee!
Thou didst create the earth according to thy will, being alone:
55.   Mankind, cattle, all flocks,
Everything on earth which walks with (its) feet,
    And what are on high, flying with their wings.

The foreign lands of Hurru and Nubia, the land of Egypt—
    Thou dost set each man in his place and supply his needs;
60. Each one has his food, and his lifetime is reckoned.
Their tongues are diverse in speech and their natures likewise;
    Their skins are varied, for thou dost vary the foreigners.
Thou dost make the Nile in the underworld,
    And bringest it forth as thou desirest to sustain the people,
65 As thou dost make them for thyself,
    Lord of them all, who dost weary thyself with them,
Lord of every land, who dost rise for them,
    Thou Aten of the day, great in majesty.

As for all distant foreign lands, thou makest their life,
70.   For thou hast set a Nile in the sky,
That it may descend for them,
    That it may make waves on the mountains like the sea,
    To water their fields amongst their towns.
How excellent are thy plans, thou lord of eternity!
75.   The Nile in the sky is for the foreign peoples,
For the flocks of every foreign land that walk with (their) feet,
    While the (true) Nile comes forth from the underworld for
        Egypt.

Thy rays suckle every field;
    When thou dost rise, they live and thrive for thee.
80. Thou makest the seasons to nourish all that thou hast made:
    The winter to cool them; the heat that they (?) may taste thee.
Thou didst make the distant sky to rise in it,
    To see all that thou hast made.
Being alone, and risen in thy form as the living Aten,
85. Whether appearing, shining, distant, or near,
Thou makest millions of forms from thyself alone:
Cities, towns, fields, road, and river. . . .

There is no other that knows thee,
95. Save thy son Akhenaten,
    For thou hast made him skilled in thy plans and thy might.

The earth came into being by thy hand,
Just as thou didst make them (i.e. mankind).

When thou hast risen, they live;
100.   When thou dost set, they die.
For thou art lifetime thyself; one lives through thee;
Eyes are upon (thy) beauty until thou dost set.
All labour is put aside when thou dost set in the west;
When [thou] risest [thou] makest . . . flourish for the king.
105. As for all who hasten on foot,
Ever since thou didst fashion the earth,
Thou dost raise them up for thy son who came forth from thyself,
The King of Upper and Lower Egypt, Akhenaten.

> Introduction and translation by R. J. Williams, in
> D. Winton Thomas (ed.), Documents from Old Testa-
> ment Times (London: Thomas Nelson, 1958)

See also nos. 54, 133, 272, 273

21. VARUNA, THE ALL-KNOWING GOD

'He knows the pathway of the wind . . .'

('Rig Veda,' I, 25, 1-3, 7-14)

1. Whatever law of thine, O god, O Varuna, as we are men,
Day after day we violate,
2. Give us not as a prey to death, to be destroyed by thee in wrath,
To thy fierce anger when displeased.
3. To gain thy mercy, Varuna, with hymns we bind thy heart,
as binds
The charioteer his tethered horse. . . .
7. He knows the path of birds that fly through heaven, and,
sovereign of the sea,
He knows the ships that are thereon.
8. True to his holy law, he knows the twelve moons with their
progeny:
He knows the moon of later birth.[1]

9. He knows the pathway of the wind, the spreading, high and
    mighty wind;
    He knows the gods who dwell above.

10. Varuna, true to holy law, sits down among his people; he,
    Most wise, sits there to govern all.

11. From thence perceiving he beholds all wondrous things, both
    what hath been,
    And what hereafter will be done.

12. May that Adyita very wise, make fair paths for us all our days;
    May he prolong our lives for us,

13. Varuna, wearing golden mail, hath clad him in a shining robe;
    His spies² are seated round about.

17. The god whom enemies threaten not, nor those who tyrannize
    o'er men,
    Nor those whose minds are bent on wrong.

Notes

1 Twelve months have days as the progeny; 'the moon of later birth' is perhaps
an intercalary 'thirteenth' month. Thus is there no 'time' to which Varuna is
not a witness.
2 Perhaps the other Adityas (cf. *Rigveda*, VIII, 47, 11).

Translation by Ralph T. H. Griffith, in his *The Hymns
of the Rigveda*, I (Benares, 1889), pp. 42-3

22. 'KING VARUNA IS THERE . . .'

('Atharva Veda,' IV, 16, 1-6)

1. The great guardian among these (gods) sees as if from anear. He
that thinketh he is moving stealthily—all this the gods know.

2. If a man stands, walks, or sneaks about, if he goes slinking away,
if he goes into his hiding-place; if two persons sit together and scheme,
King Varuna is there as a third, and knows it.

3. Both this earth here belongs to King Varuna, and also yonder
broad sky whose boundaries are far away. Moreover these two oceans
are the loins of Varuna; yea, he is hidden in this small (drop of) water.

4. He that should flee beyond the heaven far away would not be free
from King Varuna. His spies¹ comes hither (to the earth) from heaven,
with a thousand eyes do they watch over the earth.

5. King Varuna sees through all that is between heaven and earth, and all that is beyond. He has counted the winkings of men's eyes. As a (winning) gamester puts down his dice, thus does he establish these (laws).[2]

6. May all thy fateful toils which, seven by seven, threefold, lie spread out, ensnare him that speaks falsehood; him that speaks the truth they shall let go!

Notes

1 Varuna's spies are the stars 'The eyes of the night' (R V, X, 127, 1) the beholders of men' (A V, XIX, 47, 3 ff.)

2 As the player plants down these (successful dice) thus does Varuna establish these laws.

Translation by Maurice Bloomfield, *Hymns of the Atharva-Veda*, in *Sacred Books of the East*, XLII (Oxford, 1897), pp. 88-9

23. VARUNA AND INDRA

('Rig Veda,' IV, 42, 1-7, 10)

1. *I am the royal ruler, mine is empire, as mine who*
   sway all life are all the immortals.
   Varuna's will the gods obey and follow. I am the
   king o'er folk of sphere sublimest.

2. *I am king Varuna. To me was given these first*
   existing high celestial powers.[1]
   Varuna's will the gods obey and follow. I am the
   king o'er the folk of the sphere sublimest.

3. *I Varuna am Indra: in their greatness, these the*
   two wide deep fairly-fashioned regions,
   These the two world-halves have I, even as Tvashtar,[2]
   knowing all beings, joined and held together.

4. *I made to flow the moisture-shedding waters, and set*
   the heaven firm in the seat of Order.[3]
   By Law, the son of Aditi,[4] Law-observer, hath spread
   abroad the world in three fold measure.

33

5. Heroes with noble horses, fain for battle, selected
   warriors, call on me in combat.
   I, Indra Maghavan,[5] excite the conflict; I stir the
   dust, lord of surpassing vigour.

6. All this I did. The gods' own conquering power
   never impedeth me to whom none opposeth.
   When lauds and Soma-juice have made me joyful,
   both the unbounded regions are affrighted.

7. All beings know these deeds of thine: thou tellest
   this unto Varuna, thou great disposer!
   Thou art renowned as having slain the Vritras. Thou
   madest flow the floods that were obstructed. . . .

10. May we, possessing much, delight in riches, gods in
    oblations and the kine in pasture;
    And that milch-cow[6] who shrinks not from the milking
    O Indra Varuna, give to us daily.

Notes

1 Varuna speaks in stanzas 1 to 4, stressing that celestial sovereignty which is rightfully his as creator of the universe and maintainer of the cosmic order (*rita*).

2 Varuna, master of *māyā (māyin)*, here identifies himself with the divine articifer, Tvashtar, who is significantly, the father of Indra and of Vritrain the later Samhitās).

3 *Rita.*

4 Varuna, son of Aditi.

5 Indra, the 'Bountiful One,' now replies in stanzas 5 and 6. His boasts of physical power, of his exploits in battle and of the 'surpassing vigour' of his generative strength, illustrate how 'might makes right' for this warrior god. He is king by force and in the following stanza (7) the poet is duly impressed with the fact that Indra has successfully challenged the sovereign lordship of Varuna.

6 I.e., wealth.

Translation by Ralph T. H. Griffith, in his *The Hymns of the Rigveda*, II (Benares, 1890), pp. 163-5

24. 'WHAT GOD SHALL WE ADORE WITH OUR OBLATION?'

('Rig Veda,' X, 121, 1-10)

1. In the beginning rose Hiranyagarbha,[1] born only lord of all created beings.

He fixed and holdeth up this earth and heaven.
What god shall we adore with our oblation?

2. Giver of vital breath, of power and vigour, he whose commandments
   all the gods acknowledge;
   Whose shade is death, whose lustre makes immortal.
   What god shall we adore with our oblation?

3. Who by his grandeur hath become sole ruler of all the moving
   world that breathes and slumbers;
   He who is lord of men and lord of cattle.
   What god shall we adore with our oblation?

4. His, through his might, are these snow-covered mountains, and
   men call sea and Rasā[2] his possession;
   His arms are these, his are these heavenly regions.
   What god shall we adore with our oblation?

5. By him the heavens are strong and earth is steadfast, by him light's
   realm and sky-vault are supported;[3]
   By him the regions in mid-air were measured.
   What god shall we adore with our oblation?

6. To him, supported by his help, two armies embattled look while
   trembling in their spirit,
   When over them the risen sun is shining.
   What god shall we adore with our oblation?

7. What time the mighty waters[4] came, containing the universal
   germ, producing Agni,
   Thence sprang the gods' one spirit[5] into being.
   What god shall we adore with our oblation?

8. He in his might surveyed the floods containing productive force
   and generating worship.[6]
   He is the god of gods, and none beside him.
   What god shall we adore with our oblation?

9. Ne'er may he harm us who is earth's begetter, nor he whose laws
   are sure, the heavens' creator,
   He who brought forth the great and lucid waters.
   What god shall we adore with our oblation?

10. Prajāpati![7] thou only comprehendest all these created things, and
    none beside thee.
    Grant us our hearts' desire when we invoke thee;
    may we have store in riches in possession.

Notes

1 The 'golden germ (garbha).' Compare the 'primal seed' (retas, semen virile) of

X, 12, 4. The refrain concluding each stanza asks, 'Who is the god whom I should worship?' The poet in this creation hymn seeks to *name* That One who is the true source of being. Later reciters, confused by the recurrent interrogaative, posited a deity named 'Ka' ('Who?') to whom this hymn was thenceforth addressed.

2 The mythological river which encompasses the earth and the atmosphere.

3 As Varuna, in his work of creation (see VII, 86, 1) propped apart heaven and earth, so here does Hiranyagarbha perform the same divisive operation, creating a mid-space (*antariksha*) in the process.

4 Again, as in X, 129, it is the primordial waters which bear creation's germ. Here the solar germ and the fire forms of Agni are generated from the waters. Hiranyagarbha and Agni are both golden sons of the waters; they portray that unique coincidence of creation-in-chaos where the bright fire glows in the lap of dark chaotic waters.

5 The living spirit (*asu*) of all the gods is manifest uniquely when Hiranygarbha comes with the flooding waters.

6 Or, generating sacrifice.

7 Lord of creatures, the answer to the interrogative refrain. This is an important text for the later Brāhmanas, where Prajāpati is identical with the sacrifice and 'creates the all out of himself.'

Translation by Ralph T. H. Griffith, in his *The Hymns of the Rigveda*, IV (Benares, 1892), pp. 355-6

25. 'INDRA—WHO AS SOON AS BORN SURPASSED THE GODS IN POWER'

('Rig Veda,' II, 12, 1-5, 13)

1. *The chief wise god who as soon as born*
   surpassed the gods in power;
   Before whose vehemence the two worlds trembled by reason
   of the greatness of his valour: he, O men, is, Indra.[1]

2. *Who made firm the quaking earth,*
   who set at rest the agitated mountains;
   Who measures out the air more widely,
   who supported heaven: he, O men, is Indra.

3. *Who having slain the serpent released the seven streams,*
   who drove out the cows by the unclosing of Vala,
   Who between two rocks has produced fire,
   victor in battles: he, O men, is Indra.[2]

4. *By whom all things here have been made unstable,*[3]

who has made subject the Dāsa colour[4] and has made it
disappear;
Who, like a sinning gambler the stake,
has taken the possessions of the foe: he, O men, is Indra.
5. The terrible one of whom they ask 'where is he,'
of whom they also say 'he is not';
He diminishes the possessions of the foe like the stakes of
gamblers. Believe in him: he, O men, is Indra. . . .
13. Even Heaven and Earth bow down before him;[5]
before his vehemence even the mountains are afraid.
Who is known as the Soma-drinker, holding the bolt in his arm,
who holds the bolt in his hand: he, O men, is Indra.[6]

Notes

1 In contrast with Varuna and the *asuras*, another group of gods, the *devas*,
is led by Indra, the warrior god, who is king (*svarāj*) not like Varuna through
the evolving cosmic order, but rather by virtue of his own dynamic being.
2 Here the famous exploits of Indra are recalled: the slaying of the serpent
Vritra, who encompassed the cosmic waters, released for men the seven rivers
(see *Rig Veda* I, 32); Vala, another demon and the brother of Vritra, was also
slain by Indra; and Agni as lightning was generated by Indra from the clouds,
as fire is struck from flint. All of Indra's effusive deeds are the result of his
generative bull-like nature.
3 *Cyavanā*, 'shaking'; the advent of Indra's power has calmed earthquakes
(stanza 2) but has agitated and made transient all worldly phenomena.
4 The non-Aryan population.
5 Gradually in the *Rig Veda* Indra takes over those roles which formerly had
been Varuna's, until eventually Indra too achieves sovereignty. (cf. *Rig Veda*
IV, 42 and X, 124.)
6 Indra is the greatest drinker of intoxicating *soma*. The *vajra*, his thunderbolt,
is in constant use against his foes.

> Translation by A. A. Macdonell, in his *A Vedic Reader
> for Students* (Oxford: Clarendon Press, 1917), pp. 45-54,
> *passim* (slightly modified)

See also nos. 56, 101, 115, 134-7

26. A VEDIC HYMN TO THE GODDESS EARTH

('Atharva Veda,' XII, 1, selections)

1. Truth, greatness, universal order *(rita)*, strength, consecration,
creative fervour *(tapas)*, spiritual exaltation *(brahman)*, the sacrifice,

support the earth. May this earth, the mistress of that which was and shall be, prepare for us a broad domain!

2. The earth that has heights, and slopes, and great plains, that supports the plants of manifold virtue, free from the pressure that comes from the midst of men, she shall spread out for us, and fit herself for us!

3. The earth upon which the sea, and the rivers and the waters, upon which food and the tribes of men have arisen, upon which this breathing, moving life exists, shall afford us precedence in drinking!

4. The earth whose are the four regions of space upon which food and the tribes of men have arisen, which supports the manifold breathing, moving things, shall afford us cattle and other possessions also!

5. The earth upon which of old the first men[1] unfolded themselves, upon which the gods overcame the Asuras,[2] shall procure for us (all) kinds of cattle, horses, and fowls, good fortune, and glory!

6. The earth that supports all, furnishes wealth, the foundation, the golden breasted resting-place of all living creatures, she that supports Agni Vaishvānara,[3] and mates with Indra, the bull,[4] shall furnish us with property!

7. The broad earth, which the sleepless gods ever attentively guard, shall milk for us precious honey, and, moreover, besprinkle us with glory!

8. That earth which formerly was water upon the ocean (of space), which the wise (seers) found out by their skilful devices;[5] whose heart is in the highest heaven, immortal, surrounded by truth, shall bestow upon us brilliancy and strength, (and place us) in supreme sovereignty! . . .

10. The earth which the Ashvins[6] have measured, upon which Vishnu[7] has stepped out, which Indra, the lord of might, has made friendly to himself; she, the mother, shall pour forth milk for me, the son!

11. Thy snowy mountain heights, and thy forests, O earth, shall be kind to us! The brown, the black, the red, the multi-coloured, the firm earth, that is protected by Indra, I have settled upon, not suppressed, not slain, not wounded.

12. Into thy middle set us, O earth, and into thy navel, into the nourishing strength that has grown up from thy body; purify thyself for us! The earth is the mother, and I the son of the earth: Parjanya[8] is the father; he, too, shall save us!

13. The earth upon which they (the priests) inclose the altar *(vedi)*, upon which they, devoted to all (holy) works, unfold the sacrifice, upon which are set up, in front of the sacrifice, the sacrificial posts, erect and brilliant, that earth shall prosper us, herself prospering!

14. Him that hates us, O earth, him that battles against us, him that is hostile towards us with his mind and his weapons, do thou subject to us, anticipating (our wish) by deed!

15. The mortals born of thee live on thee, thou supportest both bipeds and quadrupeds. Thine, O earth, are these five races of men, the mortals, upon whom the rising sun sheds undying light with his rays. . . .

22. Upon the earth men give to the gods the sacrifice, the prepared oblation: upon the earth mortal men live pleasantly by food. May this earth give us breath and life, may she cause me to reach old age!

23. The fragrance, O earth, that has arisen upon thee, which the plants and the waters hold, which the Gandharvas and the Apsaras[9] have partaken of, with that make me fragrant: not any one shall hate us! . . .

40. May this earth point out to us the wealth that we crave: may Bhaga (fortune) add his help, may Indra come here as (our) champion!

41. The earth upon whom the noisy mortals sing and dance, upon whom they fight, upon whom resounds the roaring drum, shall drive forth our enemies, shall make us free from rivals!

42. To the earth upon whom are food, and rice and barley, upon whom live these five races of men, to the earth, the wife of Parjanya, that is fattened by rain, be reverence!

43. The earth upon whose ground the citadels constructed by the gods unfold themselves, every region of her that is the womb of all, Prajāpati[10] shall make pleasant for us! . . .

45. The earth that holds people of manifold varied speech, of different customs, according to their habitations, as a reliable milch-cow that does not kick, shall she milk for me a thousand streams of wealth!

46. The serpent, the scorpion with thirsty fangs, that hibernating torpidly lies upon thee; the worm, and whatever living thing, O earth, moves in the rainy season, shall, when it creeps not creep upon us; with what is auspicious (on thee) be gracious to us! . . .

48. The earth holds the fool and holds the wise, endures that good and bad dwell (upon her); she keeps company with the boar, gives herself up to the wild hog. . . .

52. The earth upon whom day and night jointly, black and bright,

have been decreed, the broad earth covered and enveloped with rain, shall kindly place us into every pleasant abode !

53. Heaven, and earth, and air have here given me expanse: Agni, Sūrya,[11] the waters, and all the gods together have given me wisdom. . . .

63. O mother earth, kindly set me down upon a well-founded place ! With (father) heaven cooperating, O thou wise one, do thou place me into happiness and prosperity ![12]

Notes

1 *Pūrvajana*, 'men of former times.'

2 By the time of the composition of the Atharvaveda, as in the late *Rigveda*, the *asuras*, sovereign gods under Varuna's command, have become demons; the *devas* were the gods who 'overcame' them.

3 *Vaishvānara*, 'belonging to all men,' is a frequent epithet of Agni, the fire, and refers to his omnipresence.

4 Indra's fecund powers are often characterized by his bull form: here, 'the earth (*bhūmi*) whose bull is Indra.'

5 *Māyā*.

6 The divine twins, beautiful and amiable physicians among the gods, whose golden chariot traverses heaven and earth in a day.

7 Vishnu, still a minor god in the Atharvaveda, is celebrated for his three great strides: already the first of these covered the broad span of earth, the second then limited the sky, and the third encompassed transcendent space.

8 A lesser deity associated with the rain clouds and terrestrial fertility. Verse 42 calls earth his wife.

9 The Gandharvas are a class of celestial beings sometimes described as dwelling with their Apsaras nymphs in the waters on earth. [*See below, selection no. 116, the story of Purūravas, Urvashī and the lotus lake.* M.E.]

10 Lord of creatures and protector of generation.

11 The sun.

12 Vaitāna-sūtra 27.8 prescribes this verse for recitation upon descending from the sacrificial post (W. D. Whitney [trans.], *Atharva-Veda Samhitā* [ed. by C. R. Lanman], Cambridge, Mass.: Harvard University, 1905, p. 672). The hymn itself is one of the few examples of freshly inspired poetry in the Atharvaveda. 'Its chief use is at the *āgrahāyaṇi*-ceremonies, the concluding ceremonies of the rites devoted to serpents, undertaken on the full-moon day of the month Mārgashīrsha.' It is also connected with rites that firmly establish the house, homestead, or village. (Bloomfield, pp. 639-40.)

Translation by Maurice Bloomfield, *Hymns of the Atharva-Veda*, in *The Sacred Books of the East*, XLII (Oxford, 1891), pp. 199-207

See also no. 163

27. VISHNU, THE COSMIC GOD

('Vishnu Purāna,' 3, 17, 14-34)

You are everything, earth, water, fire, air, and space,
the subtle world, the Nature-of-All (pradhāna),
and the Person (pums) who stands forever aloof.

O Self of all beings!
From the Creator (Brahmā) to the blade of grass
all is your body, visible and invisible,
divided by space and time.

We worship you as Brahmā, the Immense Being, the first shape,
who sprang from the lotus of your navel to create the worlds.

We, the gods, worship you in our selves,
we, the King of Heaven, the Sun, the Lord of Tears,
the Indweller, the twin gods of agriculture,
the Lord of Wind, the Offering, who all are your shapes
while you are our Selves.

We worship you in your demonic shapes, deceitful and stupid,
wild in their passions, suspicious of wisdom.

We worship you in the genii, the yakshas,
with their narrow minds obdurate to knowledge,
their blunt faculties covetous of the objects of words.

O Supreme Man! We bow to your fearful evil shapes
which wander at night, cruel and deceitful.

O Giver-of-Rewards (Junārdana)!
We worship you as the Eternal Law
whence virtuous men, who dwell in the heaven,
obtain the blissful fruit of their just deeds.
We bow to the Realized (Siddhas) who are your shapes of joy;
free from contacts, they enter and move within all things.

O Remover-of-Sorrow (Hari)! We bow to you the serpent shapes,
lustful and cruel, whose forked tongues know no mercy.

O Pervader! We worship you as knowledge
in the peaceful form of the seers,
faultless, free from sin.

Gods, Goddesses and Supernatural Beings

O Dweller in the lotus of the Heart! We bow to you
as the self of Time which, at the end of the ages,
infallibly devours all beings.

We worship you as the Lord of Tears,
who dances at the time of destruction,
having devoured gods and men alike.

O Giver of Rewards! We worship your human shape
bound by the twenty-eight incapacities (badha),
ruled by the powers of darkness.

We bow to you as vegetal life (mukhya rūpa),
by which the world subsists and which—six in kind,
trees, [creepers, bushes, plants, herbs, and bamboo]—
supports the sacrificial rites.

O Universal Self! We bow to you under that elemental shape
from which beasts and men have sprung,
gods and living beings, ether and the elements,
sound and all the qualities.

O Transcendent Self! We bow to you as the Cause of causes,
the Principal shape beyond compare,
beyond Nature (pradhāna) and Intellect.

O All-powerful (Bhagavān)! We bow to your shape
which the seers alone perceive and in which is found
no white nor other colour, no length nor other dimension,
no density nor other quality.

Purer than purity it stands
beyond the sphere of quality.

We bow to you, the birthless, the indestructible,
outside whom there is but nothingness.

You are the ever-present within all things,
as the intrinsic principle of all.

We bow to you, resplendent Indweller (Vāsudeva)! the seed of all
    that is!
You stand changeless, unsullied.

The Supreme stage is your core, the Universe your shape.
You are the unborn, Eternal.

Translation by Alain Daniélou, in his Hindu Polytheism (New York: Bollingen Series LXXIII, 1964),
pp. 367-8

28. KRISHNA'S EPIPHANY

(Bhagavad Gītā, XI, selections)

3. Thus it is, as Thou declarest
    Thyself, O Supreme Lord.
   I desire to see Thy form
    As God, O Supreme Spirit!

4. If Thou thinkest that it can
    Be seen by me, O Lord,
   Prince of mystic power, then do Thou to me
    Reveal Thine immortal Self.

   The Blessed One said:
7. Behold My forms, son of Prtha,
    By hundreds and by thousands,
   Of various sorts, marvelous,
    Of various colours and shapes. . . .

8. But thou canst not see Me
    With this same eye of thine own;
   I give thee a supernatural eye:
    Behold My mystic power as God!

   Samjaya said:
9. Thus speaking then, O king,
    Hari (Visnu), the great Lord of Mystic Power,
   Showed unto the son of Prtha
    His supernal form as God: . . .

12. Of a thousand suns in the sky
     If suddenly should burst forth
    The light, it would be like
     Unto the light of that exalted one. . . .

14. Then filled with amazement,
     His hair standing upright, Dhanamjaya
    Bowed with his head to the God,
     And said with a gesture of reverence:

    Arjuna said:
15. I see the gods in Thy body, O God,
     All of them, and the hosts of various kinds of beings too,
    Lord Brahma sitting on the lotus-seat,
     And the seers all, and the divine serpents.

16. With many arms, bellies, mouths, and eyes,
    I see Thee, infinite in form on all sides;
    No end nor middle nor yet beginning of Thee
    Do I see, O All-God, All-formed!

17. With diadem, club, and disc,
    A mass of radiance, glowing on all sides,
    I see Thee, hard to look at, on every side
    With the glory of flaming fire and sun, immeasurable.

18. Thou art the Imperishable, the supreme Object of Knowledge;
    Thou art the ultimate resting-place of this universe;
    Thou are the immortal guardian of the eternal right.
    Thou art the everlasting Spirit, I hold.

19. Without beginning, middle, or end, of infinite power,
    Of infinite arms, whose eyes are the moon and sun,
    I see Thee, whose face is flaming fire,
    Burning this whole universe with Thy radiance.

20. For this region between heaven and earth
    Is pervaded by Thee alone, and all the directions;
    Seeing this Thy wondrous, terrible form,
    The triple world trembles, O exalted one!

21. For into Thee are entering yonder throngs of gods;
    Some, affrighted, praise Thee with reverent gestures;
    Crying 'Hail!' the throngs of the great seers and perfected ones
    Praise Thee with abundant laudations. . . .

24. Touching the sky, aflame, of many colours,
    With yawning mouths and flaming enormous eyes,
    Verily seeing Thee (so), my inmost soul is shaken,
    And I find no steadiness nor peace, O Visnu!

25. And Thy mouths, terrible with great tusks,
    No sooner do I see them, like the fire of dissolution (of the
    world),
    Than I know not the directions of the sky, and I find no refuge;
    Have mercy, Lord of Gods, Thou in whom the world dwells! . . .

31. Tell me, who art Thou, of awful form?
    Homage be to Thee: Best of Gods, be merciful!
    I desire to understand Thee, the primal one;
    For I do not comprehend what Thou hast set out to do.

The Blessed One said:

32. I am Time (Death), cause of destruction of the worlds, matured
    And set out to gather in the worlds here.
    Even without thee (thy action), all shall cease to exist,
    The warriors that are drawn up in the opposing ranks.

33. Therefore arise thou, win glory,
    Conquer thine enemies and enjoy prospered kingship;
    By Me Myself they have already been slain long ago;
    Be thou the mere instrument, left-handed archer!

34. Drona and Bhisma and Jayadratha,
    Karna too, and the other warrior-heroes as well,
    Do thou slay, (since) they are already slain by Me; do not hesitate!
    Fight! Thou shalt conquer thy rivals in battle. . . .

    Arjuna said:

36. It is in place, Hrsikesa, that at Thy praise
    The world rejoices and is exceeding glad;
    Ogres fly in terror in all directions,
    And all the hosts of perfected ones pay homage.

37. And why should they not pay homage to Thee, Exalted One?
    Thou art greater even than Brahman; Thou art the First Creator;
    O infinite Lord of Gods, in whom the world dwells,
    Thou the imperishable, existent, non-existent, and beyond both!

38. Thou art the Primal God, the Ancient Spirit,
    Thou art the supreme resting-place of this universe;
    Thou art the knower, the object of knowledge, and the highest
        station,
    By Thee the universe is pervaded, Thou of infinite form! . . .

42. And if I treated thee disrespectfully to make sport of Thee,
    In the course of amusement, resting, sitting, or eating,
    Either since, O unshaken one, or in the presence of those (others),
    For that I beg forgiveness of Thee, the immeasurable one.

43. Thou art the father of the world of things that move and move not,
    And thou art its revered, most venerable Guru;
    There is no other like Thee—how then a greater?—
    Even in the three worlds, O Thou of matchless greatness!

44. Therefore, bowing and prostrating my body,
    I beg grace of Thee, the Lord to be revered:
    As a father to his son, as a friend to his friend,
    As a lover to his beloved, be pleased to show mercy, O God!

45. *Having seen what was never seen before, I am thrilled,*
    And (at the same time) my heart is shaken with fear;
    Show me, O God, that same form of Thine (as before)!
    Be merciful, Lord of Gods, Abode of the World!

Translation by Franklin Edgerton, in Edgerton *Bhaga-vad Gītā*, Vol. I, Harvard Oriental Series, Vol. 38 (Cambridge, Harvard University Press, 1944)

29. TO EACH GENERATION THE TATHĀGATA ANNOUNCES HIS NAME AND DECLARES THAT HE HAS ENTERED NIRVĀNA

('Saddharmapundarika,' XV, 268-72)

The Buddha, considered as a spiritual principle and not as a historical person, is called 'Tathāgata.' The original meaning of the term is no longer known.

The Lord said: As a result of my sustaining power this world, with its Gods, men and Asuras, forms the notion that recently the Lord Shakyamuni, after going forth from his home among the Shakyas, has awoken to full enlightenment, on the terrace of enlightenment, by the town of Gayā.

But one should not see it thus, sons of good family. In fact it is many hundreds of thousands of myriads of Kotis of aeons ago that I have awoken to full enlightenment. . . . Ever since, during all that time I have demonstrated Dharma to beings in this Saha world system, and also in hundreds of thousands of Nayutas of Kotis of other world systems. But when I have spoken of other Tathāgatas, beginning with the Tathāgata Dīpankara, and of the Nirvāna of these Tathāgatas, then that has just been conjured up by me as an emission of the skill in means by which I demonstrate Dharma.

Moreover, the Tathāgata surveys the diversity in the faculties and vigour of successive generations of beings. To each generation he announces his name, declares that he has entered Nirvāna, and brings peace to beings by various discourses on Dharma. To beings who are of low disposition, whose store of merit is small, and whose depravities are many, he says in that case: 'I am young in years, monks, I have

46

left the home of my family, and but lately have I won full enlightenment.' But when the Tathāgata, although fully enlightened for so long, declares that he has been fully enlightened but recently, then such discourses on Dharma have been spoken for no other reason than to bring beings to maturity and to save them. All these discourses on Dharma have been taught by the Tathāgata in order to discipline beings.

And whatever the Tathāgata says to educate beings, and whatever the Tathāgata utters,—whether he appears as himself or as another, whether under his own authority or another,—all these discourses on Dharma are taught as factually true by the Tathāgata, and there is no false speech in them on the part of the Tathāgata. For the Tathāgata has seen the triple world as it really is: It is not born, it dies not; there is no decease or rebirth, no Samsāra or Nirvāna; it is not real, or unreal, not existent, or non-existent, not such, or otherwise, not false or not-false. Not in such a way has the Tathāgata seen the triple world as the foolish common people see it. The Tathāgata is face to face with the reality of dharmas; he can therefore be under no delusion about them. Whatever words the Tathāgata may utter with regard to them, they are true, not false, not otherwise.

He utters, however, different discourses on Dharma, which differ in their objective basis, to beings who differ in their mode of life and their intentions, and who wander amidst discriminations and perceptions, in order to generate the roots of good in them. For a Tathāgata performs a Tathāgata's work. Fully enlightened for ever so long, the Tathāgata has an endless span of life, he lasts for ever. Although the Tathāgata has not entered Nirvāna, he makes a show of entering Nirvāna, for the sake of those who have to be educated. And even today my ancient course as a Bodhisattva is still incomplete, and my life-span is not yet ended. From today onwards still twice as many hundreds of thousands of Nayutas of Kotis of aeons must elapse before my life-span is complete. Although therefore I do not at present enter into Nirvāna (or extinction), nevertheless I announce my Nirvāna. For by this method I bring beings to maturity. Because it might be that, if I stayed here too long and could be seen too often, beings who have performed no meritorious actions, who are without merit, a poorly lot, eager for sensuous pleasures, blind, and wrapped in the net of false views, would, in the knowledge that the Tathāgata stays (here all the time), get the notion that life is a mere sport, and would not conceive the notion that the (sight of the) Tathāgata is hard to obtain. In the conviction that the Tathāgata is always at hand they would not exert their vigour for the purpose of escaping from the triple world, and they would not conceive of the Tathāgata as hard to obtain.

Translation by Edward Conze, in Conze, *et al.*, *Buddhist Texts through the Ages* (Oxford: Bruno Cassirer, 1954)

30. THE BODHISATTVA'S INFINITE COMPASSION

(*'Shikshāsamuccaya,'* 280-2 [*'Vajradhvaha-sūtra'*])

A Bodhisattva resolves: I take upon myself the burden of all suffering. I am resolved to do so, I will endure it. I do not turn or run away, do not tremble, am not terrified, nor afraid, do not turn back or despond.

And why? At all costs I must bear the burdens of all beings. In that I do not follow my own inclinations. I have made the vow to save all beings. All beings I must set free. The whole world of living beings I must rescue, from the terrors of birth, of old age, of sickness, of death and rebirth, of all kinds of moral offence, of all states of woe, of the whole cycle of birth-and-death, of the jungle of false views, of the loss of wholesome dharmas, of the concomitants of ignorance,— from all these terrors I must rescue all beings. . . . I walk so that the kingdom of unsurpassed cognition is built up for all beings. My endeavours do not merely aim at my own deliverance. For with the help of the boat of the thought of all-knowledge, I must rescue all these beings from the stream of Samsāra, which is so difficult to cross, I must pull them back from the great precipice, I must free them from all calamities, I must ferry them across the stream of Samsāra. I myself must grapple with the whole mass of suffering of all beings. To the limit of my endurance I will experience in all the states of woe, found in any world system, all the abodes of suffering. And I must not cheat all beings out of my store of merit, I am resolved to abide in each single state of woe for numberless aeons; and so I will help all beings to freedom, in all the states of woe that may be found in any world system whatsoever.

And why? Because it is surely better that I alone should be in pain than that all these beings should fall into the states of woe. There I must give myself away as a pawn through which the whole world is redeemed from the terrors of the hells, of animal birth, of the world of Yama, and with this my own body I must experience, for the sake of all beings, the whole mass of all painful feelings. And on behalf of all beings I give surety for all beings, and in doing so I speak truthfully, am trustworthy, and do not go back on my word. I must not abandon all beings.

And why? There has arisen in me the will to win all-knowledge, with all beings for its object, that is to say, for the purpose of setting free the entire world of beings. And I have not set out for the supreme enlightenment from a desire for delights, not because I hope to experience the delights of the five-sense qualities, or because I wish to indulge in the pleasures of the senses. And I do not pursue the course of a Bodhisattva in order to achieve the array of delights that can be found in the various worlds of sense-desire.

And why? Truly no delights are all these delights of the world. All this indulging in the pleasures of the senses belongs to the sphere of Māra.

Translation by Edward Conze, in Conze, *et al.*, *Buddhist Texts through the Ages* (Oxford: Bruno Cassirer, 1954)

31. THE SUN GODDESS AMATERASU AND THE STORM GOD SUSA-NO-O

('Nihongi,' I, 40-5)

In Japanese tradition, Amaterasu and Susa-no-o were the two most important among many offspring of the primordial pair, Izanagi and Izanami.

After this Susa-no-o Mikoto's behaviour was exceedingly rude. In what way? Amaterasu [the Heaven-shining Deity] had made august rice fields of Heavenly narrow rice fields and Heavenly long rice fields. Then Susa-no-o, when the seed was sown in spring, broke down the divisions between the plots of rice, and in autumn let loose the Heavenly piebald colts, and made them lie down in the midst of the rice fields. Again, when he saw that Amaterasu was about to celebrate the feast of first-fruits, he secretly voided excrement in the New Palace. Moreover, when he saw that Amaterasu was in her sacred weaving hall, engaged in weaving garments of the Gods, he flayed a piebald colt of Heaven, and breaking a hole in the roof-tiles of the hall, flung it in. Then Amaterasu started with alarm, and wounded herself with the shuttle. Indignant of this, she straightway entered the Rock-cave of Heaven, and having fastened the Rock-door, dwelt there in seclusion. Therefore constant darkness prevailed on all sides, and the alternation of night and day was unknown.

Then the eighty myriads of Gods met on the bank of the Tranquil River of Heaven, and considered in what manner they should supplicate her. Accordingly Omoi-kane[1] no Kami, with profound device and far-reaching thought, at length gathered long-singing birds[2] of the Eternal Land and made them utter their prolonged cry to one another. Moreover he made Ta-jikara-o[3] to stand beside the Rock door. Then Ame no Koyane no Mikoto, ancestor of the Nakatomi Deity Chieftains, and Futo-dama no Mikoto, ancester of the Imibe Chieftains, dug up a five-hundred branched True Sakaki tree of the Heavenly Mt. Kagu. On its upper branches they hung an august five-hundred string of Yasaka jewels. On the middle branches they hung an eight-hand mirror.[4] . . .

On its lower branches they hung blue soft offerings and white soft offerings. Then they recited their liturgy together.

Moreover Ama no Uzume[5] no Mikoto, ancestress of the Sarume[6] Chieftain, took in her hand a spear wreathed with Eulalia grass, and standing before the door of the Rock-cave of Heaven, skilfully performed a mimic dance.[7] She took, moreover, the true Sakaki tree of the Heavenly Mount Kagu, and made of it a head-dress, she took club-moss and made of it braces, she kindled fires, she placed a tub bottom upwards,[8] and gave forth a divinely-inspired utterance.

Now Amaterasu heard this, and said: 'Since I have shut myself up in the Rock-cave, there ought surely to be continual night in the Central Land of fertile reed-plains. How then can Ama no Uzume no Mikoto be so jolly?' So with her august hand, she opened for a narrow space the Rock-door and peeped out. Then Ta-jikara-o no Kami forthwith took Amaterasu by the hand and led her out. Upon this the Gods Nakatomi no Kami and Imibe no Kami at once drew a limit by means of a bottom-tied rope[9] (also called a left-hand rope) and begged her not to return again [into the cave].

After this all the Gods put the blame on Susa-no-o, and imposed on him a fine of one thousand tables,[10] and so at length chastised him. They also had his hair plucked out, and made him therewith expiate his guilt.

Gods of the Ancient Near East

Notes

1 Thought-combining or thought-including.
2 The cock is meant.
3 Hand-strength-male.
4 It is said to be this mirror which is worshipped at Ise as an emblem of the Sun Goddess.
5 Terrible female of Heaven.
6 Monkey-female.
7 This is said to be the origin of the kagura or pantomime dance performed at Shinto festivals.
8 The Nihongi strangely omits to say that, as we learn from the Kojiki, she danced on this and made it give out a sound.
9 A rope made of straw of rice which has been pulled up by the roots.
10 By tables are meant tables of offerings.

Adapted from Aston's translation of Nihongi by Wm. Theodore de Bary (ed.), Sources of Japanese Tradition (New York: Columbia University Press, 1958), pp. 29-31; notes by de Bary

C. GREEK GODS AND HEROES, AND THE IRANIAN SUPREME BEING, AHURA-MAZDA

32. TO PYTHIAN APOLLO

('The Homeric Hymns,' III, 179 ff.)

O Lord, Lycia is yours and lovely Maeonia and Miletus, charming city by the sea, but over Delos you greatly reign your own self.

Leto's all-glorious son goes to rocky Pytho, playing upon his hollow lyre, clad in divine, perfumed garments; and at the touch of the golden key his lyre sings sweet. Thence, swift as thought, he speeds from earth to Olympus, to the house of Zeus, to join the gathering of the other gods: then straightway the undying gods think only of the lyre and song, and all the Muses together, voice sweetly answering voice, hymn the unending gifts the gods enjoy and the sufferings of men, all that they endure at the hands of the deathless gods, and how they live witless and helpless and cannot find healing for death or defence against old age. Meanwhile the rich-tressed races and cheerful Seasons dance with Harmonia and Hebe and Aphrodite, daughter of Zeus, holding each other by the wrist. And among them sings one, not mean nor puny, but tall to look upon and enviable in mien, Artemis who delights in arrows, sister of Apollo. Among them sport Ares and the keen-eyed Slayer of Argus, while Apollo plays his lyre stepping high and featly and a radiance shines around him, the gleaming of his feet and close-woven vest. And they, even gold-tressed Leto, and wise Zeus, rejoice in their great hearts as they watch their dear son playing among the undying gods.

How then shall I sing of you—though in all ways you are a worthy theme for song? Shall I sing of you as wooer and in the fields of love, how you went wooing the daughter of Azan along with god-like Ischys the son of well-horsed Elatius, or with Phorbas sprung from Triops, or with Ereutheus, or with Leucippus and the wife of Leucippus . . . you on foot, he with his chariot, yet he fell not short of Triops. Or shall I sing how at the first you went about the earth seeking a place of oracle for men, O far-shooting Apollo? To Pieria first you went

52

down from Olympus and passed by sandy Lectus and Enienae and through the land of the Perrhaebi. Soon you came to Iolcus and set foot on Cenaeum in Euboea, famed for ships: you stood in the Lelantine plain, but it pleased not your heart to make a temple there and wooded groves. . . .

And further still you went, O far-shooting Apollo, and came to Onchestus, Poseidon's bright grove: there the new-broken colt distressed with drawing the trim chariot gets spirit again, and the skilled driver springs from his car and goes on his way. . . .

Then you went towards Telphusa: and there the pleasant place seemed fit for making a temple and wooded grove. You came very near and spoke to her: 'Telphusa, here I am minded to make a glorious temple, and oracle for men, and hither they will always bring perfect hecatombs, both those who live in rich Peloponnesus and those of Europe all the wave-washed isles, coming to seek oracles. And I will deliver to them all counsel that cannot fail, giving answer in my rich temple.'

So said Phoebus Apollo, and laid out all the foundations throughout, wide and very long. But when Telphusa saw this, she was angry in heart and spoke, saying: 'Lord Phoebus, worker from afar, I will speak a word of counsel to your heart, since you are minded to make here a glorious temple to be an oracle for men who will always bring hither perfect hecatombs for you; yet I will speak out, and do you lay up my words in your heart. The trampling of swift horses and the sound of mules watering at my sacred springs will always irk you, and men like better to gaze at the well-made chariots and stamping, swift-footed horses than at your great temple and the many treasures that are within. But if you will be moved by me—for you, lord, are stronger and mightier than I, and your strength is very great—build at Crisa below the glades of Parnassus: there no bright chariot will clash, and there will be no noise of swift-footed horses near your well-built altar. But so the glorious tribes of men will bring gifts to you as Iepaeon ("Hail-Healer"), and you will receive with delight rich sacrifices from the people dwelling round about.' So said Telphusa, that she alone, and not the Far-Shooter, should have renown there; and she persuaded the Far-Shooter.

Further yet you went, far-shooting Apollo, until you came to the town of the presumptous Phlegyae who dwell on this earth in a lovely glade near the Cephisian lake, caring not for Zeus. And thence you went . . . to Crisa beneath snowy Parnassus, a foothill turned towards the west: a cliff hangs over it from above, and a hollow, rugged glade runs under. There the lord Phoebus Apollo resolved to make his lovely temple, and thus he said:

'In this place I am minded to build a glorious temple to be an oracle for men, and here they will always bring perfect hecatombs, both they who dwell in rich Peloponnesus and the men of Europe and from all the wave-washed isles, coming to question me. And I will deliver to them all counsel that cannot fail, answering them in my rich temple.'

When he had said this, Phoebus Apollo laid out all the foundations throughout, wide and very long; and upon these the sons of Erginus, Trophonius and Agamedes, dear to the deathless gods, laid a footing of stone. And the countless tribes of men built the whole temple of wrought stones, to be sung of for ever.

But near by was a sweet flowing spring, and there with his strong bow the lord, the son of Zeus, killed the bloated, great-she-dragon, a fierce monster wont to do great mischief to men upon earth, to men themselves and to their thin-shanked sheep; for she was a very bloody plague. She it was who once received from gold-throned Hera and brought up fell, cruel Typhaon to be a plague to men. Once on a time Hera bare him because she was angry with father Zeus, when the son of Cronos bare all-glorious Athena in his head. . . .

And this Typhaon used to work great mischief among the famous tribes of men. Whosoever met the dragoness, the day of doom would sweep him away, until the lord Apollo, who deals death from afar, shot a strong arrow at her. Then she, rent with bitter pangs, lay drawing great gasps for breath and rolling about that place. An awful noise swelled up unspeakable as she writhed continually this way and that amid the wood: and so she left her life, breathing it forth in blood. Then Phoebus Apollo boasted over her:

'Now rot here upon the soil that feeds man! You at least shall live no more to be a fell bane to men who eat the fruit of the all-nourishing earth, and who will bring hither perfect hecatombs. Against cruel death neither Typhoeus shall avail you nor ill-famed Chimera, but here shall the Earth and shining Hyperion make you rot.'

Thus said Phoebus, exulting over her: and darkness covered her eyes. And the holy strength of Helios made her rot away there: wherefore the place is now called Pytho, and men call the lord Apollo by another name, Pythian; because on that spot the power of piercing Helios made the monster rot away.

Then Phoebus Apollo saw that the sweet-flowing spring had beguiled

him, and he started out in anger against Telphusa; and soon coming
to her, he stood close by and spoke to her:

'Telphusa, you were not, after all, to keep to yourself this lovely
place by deceiving my mind, and pour forth your clear flowing water:
here my renown shall also be and not yours alone.'

Thus spoke the lord, far-working Apollo, and pushed over upon her
a crag with a shower of rocks, hiding her streams: and he made
himself an altar in a wooded grove very near the clear-flowing stream.
In that place all men pray to the great one by the name Telphusian,
because he humbled the stream of holy Telphusa.

> Translation by Hugh G. Evelyn-White, in the Loeb
> Classical Library (New York, 1914), pp. 337 *ff*.

See also nos. 139, 304

33. THE EARTH, MOTHER OF ALL

('The Homeric Hymns,' xxx)

I will sing of well-founded Earth, mother of all, eldest of all beings.
She feeds all creatures that are in the world, all that go upon the
goodly land, and all that are in the paths of the seas, and all that fly:
all these are fed of her store. Through you, O queen, men are blessed
in their children and blessed in their harvests, and to you it belongs
to give means of life to mortal men and to take it away. Happy is
the man whom you delight to honour! He has all things abundantly:
his fruitful land is laden with corn, his pastures are covered with
cattle, and his house is filled with good things. Such men rule orderly
in their cities of fair women: great riches and wealth follow them:
their sons exult with everfresh delight, and their daughters with flower-
laden hands play and skip merrily over the soft flowers of the field.
Thus it is with those whom you honour O holy goddess, bountiful
spirit.

Hail, Mother of the gods, wife of starry Heaven; freely bestow upon
me for this my song substance that cheers the heart! And now I
will remember you and another song also.

> Translation by Hugh G. Evelyn-White, in the Loeb
> Classical Library (New York, 1914), p. 456

See also nos. 59, 148

34. HERCULES: HIS LABOURS, HIS DEATH, HIS APOTHEOSIS

(Apollodorus, 'The Library,' II; IV, 8—VII, 7)

. . . But before Amphitryon reached Thebes, Zeus came by night and prolonging the one night threefold he assumed the likeness of Amphitryon and bedded with Alcmena and related what had happened concerning the Teleboans. But when Amphitryon arrived and saw that he was not welcomed by his wife, he inquired the cause; and when she told him that he had come the night before and slept with her, he learned from Tiresias how Zeus had enjoyed her. And Alcmena bore two sons, to wit, Hercules, whom she had by Zeus and who was the elder by one night, and Iphicles, whom she had by Amphitryon. When the child was eight months old, Hera desired the destruction of the babe and sent two huge serpents to the bed. Alcmena called Amphitryon to her help, but Hercules arose and killed the serpents by strangling them with both his hands. However, Pherecydes says that it was Amphitryon who put the serpents in the bed, because he would know which of the two children was his, and that when Iphicles fled, and Hercules stood his ground, he knew that Iphicles was begotten of his body.

Hercules was taught to drive a chariot by Amphitryon, to wrestle by Autolycus, to shoot with the bow by Eurytus, to fence by Castor, and to play the lyre by Linus. This Linus was a brother of Orpheus; he came to Thebes and became a Theban, but was killed by Hercules with a blow of the lyre; for being struck by him, Hercules flew into a rage and slew him. When he was tried for murder, Hercules quoted a law of Rhadamanthys, who laid it down that whoever defends himself against a wrongful aggressor shall go free, and so he was acquitted. But fearing he might do the like again, Amphitryon sent him to the cattle farm; and there he was nurtured and outdid all in stature and strength. Even by the look of him it was plain that he was a son of Zeus; for his body measured four cubits, and he flashed a gleam of fire from his eyes; and he did not miss, neither with the bow nor with the javelin.

While he was with the herds and had reached his eighteenth year he slew the lion of Cithaeron, for that animal, sallying from Cithaeron, harried the kine of Amphitryon and of Thespius. Now this Thespius was king of Thespiae, and Hercules went to him when he wished to catch the lion. The king entertained him for fifty days, and each night, as Hercules went forth to the hunt, Thespius bedded one of his daughters with him (fifty daughters having been borne to him by Megamede, daughter of Arneus); for he was anxious that all of them should have children by Hercules. Thus Hercules, though he thought that his bedfellow was always the same, had intercourse with them all. And having vanquished the lion, he dressed himself in the skin and wore the scalp as a helmet. . . .

Having first learned from Eurytus the art of archery, Hercules received a sword from Hermes, a bow and arrows from Apollo, a golden breastplate from Hephaestus, and a robe from Athena; for he had himself cut a club at Nemea.

Now it came to pass that after the battle with the Minyans Hercules was driven mad through the jealousy of Hera and flung his own children, whom he had by Megara, and two children of Iphicles into the fire; wherefore he condemned himself to exile, and was purified by Thespius, and repairing to Delphi he inquired to the god where he should dwell. The Pythian priestess then first called him Hercules, for hitherto he was called Alcides. And she told him to dwell in Tiryns, serving Eurystheus for twelve years and to perform the ten labours imposed on him, and so, she said, when the tasks were accomplished, he would be immortal.

When Hercules heard that, he went to Tiryns and did as he was bid by Eurystheus. First, Eurystheus ordered him to bring the skin of the Nemean lion; now that was an invulnerable beast begotten by Typhon. . . . And having come to Nemea and tracked the lion, he first shot an arrow at him, but when he perceived that the beast was invulnerable, he heaved up his club and made after him. And when the lion took refuge in a cave with two mouths, Hercules built up the one entrance and came in upon the beast through the other, and putting his arm round its neck held it tight till he had choked it; so laying it on his shoulders he carried it to Cleonae. . . .

As a second labour he ordered him to kill the Lernaean hydra. That creature, bred in the swamp of Lerna, used to go forth into the plain and ravage both the cattle and the country. Now the hydra had a huge body, with nine heads, eight mortal, but the middle one immortal. So mounting a chariot driven by Iolaus, he came to Lerna, and having halted his horses, he discovered the hydra on a hill beside the springs of the Amymone, where was its den. By pelting it with fiery shafts he forced it to come out, and in the act of doing so he seized and held it fast. But the hydra wound itself about one of his feet and clung to him. Nor could he effect anything by smashing its heads with his club, for as fast as one head was smashed there grew up two. A huge crab also came to the help of the hydra by biting his foot. So he killed it, and in his turn called for help on Iolaus who, by setting fire to a piece of the neighbouring wood and burning the roots of the heads with the brands, prevented them from sprouting. Having thus got the better of the sprouting heads, he chopped off the immortal head, and buried it, and put a heavy rock on it, beside the road that leads through Lerna to Elaeus. But the body of the hydra he slit up and dipped his arrows in the gall. However, Eurystheus said that this labour should not be reckoned among the ten because he had not got the better of the hydra by himself, but with the help of Iolaus.

As a third labour he ordered him to bring the Cerynitian hind alive to Mycenae. Now the hind was at Oenoe; it had golden horns and was sacred to Artemis; so wishing neither to kill nor wound it, Hercules hunted it for a whole year. But when, weary with the chase, the beast took refuge on the mountain called Artemisius, and thence passed to the river Ladon, Hercules shot it just as it was about to cross the stream, and catching it put it on his shoulders and hastened through Arcadia. But Artemis with Apollo met him, and would have wrestled the hind from him, and rebuked him for attempting to kill her sacred animal. Howbeit, by pleading necessity and laying the blame on Eurystheus, he appeased the anger of the goddess and carried the beast alive to Mycenae.

As a fourth labour he ordered him to bring the Erymanthian boar alive; now that animal ravaged Psophis, sallying from a mountain which they call Erymanthus. . . .

The fifth labour he laid on him was to carry out the dung of the cattle of Augeas in a single day. Now Augeas was king of Elis; some say that he was a son of the Sun, others that he was a son of Poseidon, and others that he was a son of Phorbas; and he had many herds of cattle. Hercules accosted him, and without revealing the command of Eurystheus, said that he would carry out the dung in one day, if Augeas would give him the tithe of the cattle. Augeas was incredulous, but promised. Having taken Augeas's son Phyleus to witness, Hercules made a breach in the foundations of the cattle-yard, and then, diverting the courses of the Alpheus and Peneus, which flowed near each other, he turned them into the yard, having first made an outlet for the water through another opening. . . .

The sixth labour he enjoined on him was to chase away the Stymphalian birds. Now at the city of Stymphalus in Arcadia was the lake called Stymphalian, embosomed in a deep wood. To it countless birds had flocked for refuge, fearing to be preyed upon by the wolves. So when Hercules was at a loss how to drive the birds from the wood, Athena gave him brazen castanets, which she had received from Hephaestus. By clashing these on a certain mountain that overhung the lake, he scared the birds. They could not abide the sound, but fluttered up in a fright, and in that way Hercules shot them.

The seventh labour he enjoined on him was to bring the Cretan Bull. Acusilaus says that this was the bull that ferried across Europa for Zeus; but some say it was the bull that Poseidon sent up from the sea when Minos promised to sacrifice to Poseidon what should appear out of the sea. And they say that when he saw the beauty of the bull he sent it away to the herds and sacrificed another to Poseidon; at which the god was angry and made the bull savage. To attack this bull Hercules came to Crete, and when, in reply to his request for aid, Minos told him to fight and catch the bull for himself, he caught it and brought it to Eurystheus, and having shown it to him he let it afterwards go free. But the bull roamed to Sparta and all Arcadia, and traversing the Isthmus arrived at Marathon in Attica and harried the inhabitants.

The eighth labour he enjoined on him was to bring the mares of Diomedes the Thracian to Mycenae. . . .

The ninth labour he enjoined on Hercules was to bring the belt of Hippolyte. She was queen of the Amazons, who dwelt about the river Thermodon, a people great in war; for they cultivated the manly virtues, and if ever they gave birth to children through intercourse with the other sex, they reared the females; and they pinched off the right breasts that they might not be trammelled by them in throwing the javelin, but they kept the left breasts, that they might suckle. Now Hippolyte had the belt of Ares in token of her superiority to all the rest. Hercules was sent to fetch this belt because Admete, daughter of Eurystheus, desired to get it. So taking with him a band of volunteer comrades in a single ship he set sail and put it to the island of Paros, which was inhabited by the sons of Minos, to wit, Eurymedon, Chryses, Nephalion, and Philolaus. . . .

Having put in at the harbour of Themiscyra, he received a visit from Hippolyte, who inquired why he was come, and promised to give him the belt. But Hera in the likeness of an Amazon went up and down the multitude saying that the strangers who had arrived were carrying off the queen. So the Amazons in arms charged on horseback down on the ship. But when Hercules saw them in arms, he suspected treachery, and killing Hippolyte stripped her of her belt. And after fighting the rest he sailed away and touched at Troy. . . .

As a tenth labour he was ordered to fetch the kine of Geryon from Erythia. Now Erythia was an island near the ocean; it is now called Gadira. This island was inhabited by Geryon, son of Chrysaor by Callirrhoe, daughter of Ocean. He had the body of three men grown together and joined in one at the waist, but parted in three from the flanks and thighs. He owned red kine, of which Eurytion was the herdsman and Orthus, the two-headed hound, begotten by Typhon on Echidna, was the watch-dog. So journeying through Europe to fetch the kine of Geryon he destroyed many wild beasts and set foot in Libya, and proceeding to Tartessus he erected as tokens of his journey two pillars over against each other at the boundaries of Europe and Libya. But being heated by the Sun on his journey, he bent his bow at the god, who in admiration of his hardihood, gave him a golden goblet in which he crossed the ocean. And having reached Erythia he lodged on Mount Abas. However the dog, perceiving him, rushed at him; but he smote it with his club, and when the herdsman Eurytion came to the help of the dog, Hercules killed him also. But Menoetes, who was there pasturing the kine of Hades, reported to Geryon what had occurred, and he, coming up with Hercules besides the river Anthemus, as he was driving away the kine, joined battle with him and was shot dead. And Hercules, embarking the kine in the goblet and sailing across to Tartessus, gave back the goblet to the Sun. . . .

When the labours had been performed in eight years and a month, Eurystheus ordered Hercules, as an eleventh labour, to fetch golden apples from the Hesperides, for he did not acknowledge the labour of the cattle of Augeas nor that of the hydra. These apples were not, as some have said, in Libya, but on Atlas among the Hyperboreans. They were presented by Earth to Zeus after his marriage with Hera, and guarded by an immortal dragon with a hundred heads, offspring of Typhon and Echidna, which spoke with many and divers sorts of voices. With it the Hesperides also were on guard, to wit, Aegle, Erythia, Hesperia, and Arethusa. . . .

And passing by Arabia he slew Emathion, son of Tithonus, and journeying through Libya to the outer sea he received the goblet from the Sun. And having crossed to the opposite mainland he shot on the Caucasus the eagle, offspring of Echidna and Typhon, that was devouring the liver of Prometheus, and he released Prometheus, after choosing for himself the bond of olive, and to Zeus he presented Chiron who, though immortal, consented to die in his stead.

Now Prometheus had told Hercules not to go himself after the apples but to send Atlas, first relieving him of the burden of the sphere; so when he was come to Atlas in the land of the Hyperboreans, he took the advice and relieved Atlas. But when Atlas had received three apples from the Hesperides, he came to Hercules, and not wishing to support the sphere he said that he would himself carry the apples to Eurystheus, and bade Hercules hold up the sky in his stead. Hercules promised to do so, but succeeded by craft in putting it on Atlas instead. For at the advice of Prometheus he begged Atlas to hold up the sky till he should put a pad on his head. When Atlas heard that, he laid the apples down on the ground and took the sphere from Hercules. And so Hercules picked up the apples and departed. But some say that he did not get them from Atlas, but that he plucked the apples himself after killing the guardian snake. And having brought the apples he gave them to Eurystheus. But he, on receiving them, bestowed them on Hercules, from whom Athena got them and conveyed them back again; for it was not lawful that they should be laid down anywhere.

A twelfth labour imposed on Hercules was to bring Cerberus from Hades. Now this Cerberus had three heads of dogs, the tail of a dragon, and on his back the heads of all sorts of snakes. When Hercules was about to depart to fetch him, he went to Eumolpus at Eleusis, wishing to be initiated. However it was not then lawful for foreigners to be initiated, since he proposed to be initiated as the adoptive son of Pylius. But not being able to see the mysteries because he had not been cleansed of the slaughter of the centaurs, he was cleansed by Eumolpus and then initiated. And having come to Tacnarum in Laconia, where is the mouth of the descent to Hades, he descended through it. But when the souls saw him, they fled, save Meleager and the Gorgon Medusa. And Hercules drew his sword against the Gorgon, as if she were alive, but he learned from Hermes that she was an empty phantom. And being come near to the gates of Hades he found Theseus and Pirithous, him who wooed Persephone in wedlock and was therefore bound fast. And when they beheld Hercules, they stretched out their hands as if they should be raised from the dead by his might. And Theseus, indeed, he took by the hand and raised up, but when he would have brought up Pirithous, the earth quaked and he let go. And he rolled away also the stone of Ascalaphus. And wishing to provide the souls with blood, he slaughtered one of the kine of

Hades. But Menoetes, son of Ceuthonymus, who tended the kine, challenged Hercules to wrestle, and, being seized round the middle, had his ribs broken; howbeit, he was let off at the request of Persephone. When Hercules asked Pluto for Cerberus, Pluto ordered him to take the animal provided he mastered him without the use of the weapons which he carried. Hercules found him at the gates of Acheron, and, cased in his cuirass and covered by the lion's skin, he flung his arms round the head of the brute, and though the dragon in its tail bit him, he never relaxed his grip and pressure till it yielded. So he carried it off and ascended through Troezen. But Demeter turned Ascalaphus into a short-eared owl, and Hercules, after showing Cerberus to Eurystheus, carried him back to Hades. . . .

. . . And having come to Calydon, Hercules wooed Deianira, daughter of Oeneus. He wrestled for her hand with Achelous, who assumed the likeness of a bull; but Hercules broke off one of his horns. So Hercules married Deianira. . . . And taking Deianira with him, he came to the river Evenus, at which the centaur Nessus sat and ferried passengers across for hire, alleging that he had received the ferry from the gods for his righteousness. So Hercules crossed the river by himself, but on being asked to pay the fare he entrusted Deianira to Nessus to carry over. But he, in ferrying her across, attempted to violate her. She cried out, Hercules heard her, and shot Nessus to the heart when he emerged from the river. Being at the point of death, Nessus called Deianira to him and said that if she would have a love-charm to operate on Hercules she should mix the seed he had dropped on the ground with the blood that flowed from the wound inflicted by the barb. She did so and kept it by her. . . .

On his arrival at Trachis he mustered an army to attack Oechalia, wishing to punish Eurytus. Being joined by Arcadians, Melians from Trachis, and Epienemidian Locrians, he slew Eurytus and his sons and took the city. After burying those of his own side who had fallen, to wit, Hippasus, son of Ceyx, and Argius and Melas, the sons of Licymnius, he pillaged the city and led Iole captive. And having put in at Cenaeum, a headland of Euboea, he built an altar of Cenaean Zeus. Intending to offer sacrifice, he sent the herald Lichas to Trachis to fetch fine raiment. From him Deianira learned about Iole, and fearing that Hercules might love that damsel more than herself, she supposed that the spilt blood of Nessus was in truth a love charm, and with it she smeared the tunic. So Hercules put it on and proceeded to offer sacrifice. But no sooner was the tunic warmed than the poison of the hydra began to corrode his skin; and on that he lifted

Lichas by the feet, hurled him down from the headland, and tore off the tunic, which clung to his body, so that his flesh was torn away with it. In such a sad plight he was carried on shipboard to Trachis: and Deianira, on learning what had happened, hanged herself. But Hercules, after charging Hyllus his elder son by Deianira, to marry Iole when he came of age, proceeded to Mount Oeta, in the Trachinian territory, and there constructed a pyre, mounted it, and gave orders to kindle it. When no one would do so, Poeas, passing by to look for his flocks, set a light to it. On him Hercules bestowed his bow. While the pyre was burning, it is said that a cloud passed under Hercules and with a peal of thunder wafted him up to heaven. Thereafter he obtained immortality, and being reconciled to Hera he married her daughter Hebe, by whom he had sons, Alexiares and Anicetus.

Translation by Sir James George Frazer, in the Loeb Classical Library, vol. I (New York, 1921), pp. 173-237, 257-73

35. DEMETER AND THE FOUNDING OF THE ELEUSINIAN MYSTERIES

('The Homeric Hymns': To Demeter, II, 185-299)

Hades has carried off Demeter's daughter, Kore. After vainly searching for her, Demeter comes to Eleusis, in disguise as an old woman, and there is received into the house of King Celeus.

Soon they came to the house of heaven-nurtured Celeus and went through the portico to where their queenly mother sat by a pillar of the close-fitted roof, holding her son, a tender scion, in her bosom. And the girls ran to her. But the goddess walked to the threshold: and her head reached the roof and she filled the doorway with a heavenly radiance. Then awe and reverence and pale fear took hold of Metaneira, and she rose up from her couch before Demeter, and bade her be seated. But Demeter, bringer of seasons and giver of perfect gifts, would not sit upon the bright couch, but stayed silent with lovely eyes cast down until careful Iambe placed a jointed seat for her and threw over it a silvery fleece. Then she sat down and held her veil in her hands before her face. A long time she sat upon the stool[1] without speaking because of her sorrow, and greeted no one by word or by sign, but rested, never smiling, and tasting neither food nor drink, because she pined with longing for her deep-bosomed daughter, until careful Iambe—who pleased her moods in aftertime also—moved the holy lady with many a quip and jest to smile and laugh and cheer her heart. Then Metaneira filled a cup with sweet wine and offered it to her; but she refused it, for she said it was not lawful for her to drink red wine, but bade them mix meal and water with soft mint and give her to drink. And Metaneira mixed the draught and gave it to the goddess as she bade. So the great queen Deo received it to observe the sacrament.[2]

And of them all, well-girded Metaneira first began to speak: 'Hail, lady! For I think you are not meanly but nobly born; truly dignity and grace are conspicuous upon your eyes as in the eyes of kings that deal justice. Yet we mortals bear perforce what the gods send us, though we be grieved; for a yoke is set upon our necks. But now, since you are come here, you shall have what I can bestow: and nurse me this child whom the gods gave me in my old age and beyond my hope, a son much prayed for. If you should bring him up until he reach the full measure of youth, any one of womankind that sees you will straightway envy you, so great reward would I give for his upbringing.'

Then rich-haired Demeter answered her: 'And to you, also, lady, all hail, and may the gods give you good! Gladly will I take the boy to my breast, as you bid me, and will nurse him. Never, I ween, through any heedlessness of his nurse shall witchcraft hurt him nor yet the Undercutter: for I know a charm far stronger than the Wood-cutter, and I know an excellent safeguard against woeful witchcraft.'

When she had so spoken, she took the child in her fragrant bosom with her divine hands: and his mother was glad in her heart. So the goddess nursed in the place Demophoon, wise Celeus' goodly son whom well-girded Metaneira bare. And the child grew like some immortal being, not fed with food nor nourished at the breast: for by day rich-crowned Demeter would anoint him with ambrosia as if he were the offspring of a god and breathe sweetly upon him as she held him in her bosom. But at night she would hide him like a brand in the heart of the fire, unknown to his dear parents. And it wrought great wonder in these that he grew beyond his age; for he was like the gods face to face. And she would have made him deathless and unaging, had not well-girded Metaneira in her heedlessness kept watch by night from her sweet-smelling chamber and spied. But she wailed and smote her two hips, because she feared for her son and was greatly distraught in her heart, so she lamented and uttered winged words:

'Demophoon, my son, the strange woman buries you deep in fire and works grief and bitter sorrow for me.'

Thus she spoke, mourning. And the bright goddess, lovely-crowned Demeter, heard her, and was wroth with her. So with her divine hands she snatched from the fire the dear son whom Metaneira had borne unhoped-for in the palace, and cast him from her to the ground, for she was terribly angry in her heart. Forthwith she said to well-girded Metaneira:

'Witless are you mortals and dull to foresee your lot, whether of good or evil, that comes upon you. For now in your heedlessness you have wrought folly past healing; for—be witness the oath of the gods, the relentless water of Styx—I would have made your dear son deathless and unaging all his days and would have bestowed on him everlasting honour, but now he can in no way escape death and the fates. Yet shall unfailing honour always rest upon him, because he lay upon my knees and slept in my arms. But, as the years move round and when he is in his prime, the sons of the Eleusinians shall ever wage war and dread strife with one another continually. Lo! I am that Demeter who has share of honour and is the greatest help and cause of joy to the undying gods and mortal men. But now, let all the people build me a great temple and an altar below it and beneath the city and its sheer wall upon a rising hillock above Callichorus. And I myself will teach my rites, that hereafter you may reverently perform them and so win the favour of my heart.'

When she had so said, the goddess changed her stature and her looks, thrusting old age away from her: beauty spread round about her and a lovely fragrance was wafted from her sweet-smelling robes, and from the divine body of the goddess a light shone afar, while golden tresses spread down over her shoulders, so that the strong house was filled with brightness as with lightning. And so she went out from the palace.

And straightway Metaneira's knees were loosed and she remained speechless for a long while and did not remember to take up her late-born son from the ground. But his sisters heard his pitiful wailing and sprang down from their well-spread beds; one of them took up the child in her arms and laid him in her bosom, while another revived the fire, and a third rushed with soft feet to bring their mother from her fragrant chamber. And they gathered about the struggling child and washed him, embracing him lovingly; but he was not comforted, because nurses and handmaids much less skilful were holding him now.

All night long they sought to appease the glorious goddess, quaking with fear. But, as dawn began to show, they told powerful Celeus all things without fail, as the lovely-crowned goddess Demeter charged them. So Celeus called the countless people to an assembly and bade them make a goodly temple for rich-haired Demeter and an altar upon the rising hillock. And they obeyed him right speedily and harkened to his voice, doing as he commanded. As for the child, he grew like an immortal being.

Notes

1 Demeter chooses the lowlier seat, supposedly as being more suitable to her assumed condition, but really because in her sorrow she refuses all comforts.
2 An act of communion—the drinking of the potion (*kykeon*) here described— was one of the most important pieces of ritual in the Eleusinian mysteries, as commemorating the sorrow of the goddess.

Translation by Hugh G. Evelyn-White, in the Loeb Classical Library (New York, 1936)

See also nos. 148, 150, 155

36. ZALMOXIS, THE GOD OF THE GETAE

(Herodotus, 'History,' IV, 93-6)

Zalmoxis (Salmoxis) was the Supreme God of the Getae (or Dacians), a Thracian people inhabiting a territory including today's Romania, but also extending farther east and northeast. Our only important information concerning this rather enigmatic deity is the text of Herodotus quoted below. The scholars have interpreted Zalmoxis as a Sky-god, a god of the dead, a Mystery-god, etc.

93. But before he came to the Ister, he first subdued the Getae, who pretend to be immortal. The Thracians of Salmydessus and of the country above the towns of Appolonia and Mesambria, who are called

Cyrmaianae and Nipsaei, surrendered themselves unresisting to Darius; but the Getae, who are the bravest and most law-abiding of all Thracians, resisted with obstinacy, and were enslaved forthwith.

94. As to their claim to be immortal, this is how they show it: they believe that they do not die, but that he who perishes goes to the god Salmoxis of Gebelexis, as some of them call him. Once in every five years they choose by lot one of their people and send him as a messenger to Salmoxis, charged to tell of their needs; and this is their manner of sending: Three lances are held by men thereto appointed; others seize the messenger to Salmoxis by his hands and feet, and swing and hurl him aloft on to the spear-point. If he be killed by the cast, they believe that the gods regard them with favour; but if he be not killed, they blame the messenger himself, deeming him a bad man, and send another messenger in place of him whom they blame. It is while the man yet lives that they charge him with the message. Moreover when there is thunder and lightning these same Thracians shoot arrows skyward as a threat to the god, believing in no other god but their own.

95. For myself, I have been told by the Greeks who dwell beside the Hellespont and Pontus that this Salmoxis was a man who was once a slave in Samos, his master being Pythagoras, son of Mnesarchus; presently, after being freed and gaining great wealth, he returned to his own country. Now the Thracians were a meanly-living and simple-witted folk, but this Salmoxis knew Ionian usages and a fuller way of life than the Thracian; for he had consorted with Greeks, and more-over with one of the greatest Greek teachers, Pythagoras; wherefore he made himself a hall, where he entertained and feasted the chief among his countrymen, and taught them that neither he nor his guests nor any of their descendants should ever die, but that they should go to a place where they would live for ever and have all good things. While he was doing as I have said and teaching this doctrine, he was all the while making him an underground chamber. When this was finished, he vanished from the sight of the Thracians, and descended into the underground chamber, where he lived for three years, the Thracians wishing him back and mourning him for dead; then in the fourth year he appeared to the Thracians, and thus they came to believe what Salmoxis had told them. Such is the Greek story about him.

96. For myself, I neither disbelieve nor fully believe the tale about Salmoxis and his underground chamber; but I think that he lived many years before Pythagoras; and whether there was a man called Salmoxis,

or this be the name among the Getae for a god of their country, I have done with him.

Translation by A. D. Godley, in the Loeb Classical Library, vol. II (New York, 1938)

37. ZARATHUSTRA PRESENTS A 'SUMMARY OF THE DOCTRINE'

('*Gāthā:Yasna*' 45)

This *Gāthā:Yasna* 45 is addressed to the 'great public,' or at least to an unaccustomed audience. As always, the cosmogony is explained in accordance with the eschatology which is its fount and origin. Thus the opening stanza already contains a reference to the 'second existence,' the renewed existence.

1. *I will speak; hear now and attend,*
   You who from nearby or from afar come for instruction,
   Do you all make your wisdom of him, for he is manifest.
   May the false teacher not destroy the second existence.
   Who for his evil choice has been reckoned wicked, through the
      tongue.

2. *I will speak of the two spirits*
   Of whom the holier said unto the destroyer at the beginning of
      existence:
   'Neither our thoughts nor our doctrines nor our minds' forces,
   Neither our choices nor our words nor our deeds,
   Neither our consciences nor our souls agree.'

3. *I will speak of the beginnings of this existence,*
   Of the things which the Wise Lord has told me, he who knows.
   Those of you who do not carry out the word
   As I shall think it and speak it,
   For them the end of existence shall be 'Woe!'

4. *I will speak of the things which are best in this existence.*
   He who created it according to Righteousness,
   I know, O Wise One, he is the father of the active Good Mind,
   Whose daughter is beneficent Devotion.
   Not to be deceived is the all-divining Lord.

5. I will speak of the word which the Most Holy Wise Lord
   Has told me as the best for mankind to hear:
   'Those who for me shall give heed and obedience to him,
   Shall attain integrity and Immortality through the deeds of Good
   Mind.'

6. I will speak of the greatest of all,
   Praising him as Righteousness, who is benevolent towards the
   living.
   Let the Wise lord hear, as the Holy Spirit,
   Whom I have praised when I took counsel with the Good Mind!
   By his mind's force may he teach me the supreme good,

7. He who gives salvation or perdition
   To those who are living or have been or shall be:
   The soul of the righteous rewarded with Immortality,
   Everlasting torments for the wicked.
   (Of these torments also is the Wise Lord the creator, through his
   Dominion.)

   (Listeners:)
8. 'Seek to win him for us by praises of veneration
   —For I have now beheld this with mine eye,
   Knowing the Wise Lord by the Righteousness of his Good Spirit,
   Of his good deed and his good word—
   And may we offer him hymns of praise in the house of song!

9. 'Seek to propitiate him for us with the Good Mind,
   Him who gives us fortune and misfortune at will.
   May the Wise Lord through his Dominion over the village,
   Through the intimacy of the Good Mind with Righteousness,
   Prosper our cattle and our men!

10. 'Seek to glorify him for us with hymns of Devotion,
    Him who is beheld in the soul as the Wise Lord,
    Because he has promised with his Righteousness and his Good
    Mind
    That Integrity and Immortality shall be ours in his Dominion,
    Strength and endurance in his house!'

    (Zarathustra:)
11. Whoever (?therefore?) shall henceforth bear ill-will to the false
    gods
    And to those who bear ill-will to the saviour

(That is, to those who shall not submit themselves to him),
To him shall the holy conscience of the coming saviour, the master
  of his house,
Stand in stead of sworn friend, of brother or father, O Wise Lord!

Translation and introductory note by Jacques
Duchesne-Guillemin, in his *The Hymns of Zarathustra*
(London, 1952), pp 90-7

See also nos. 60, 290, 303

38. GĀTHĀ OF THE CHOICE: ZARATHUSTRA REVEALS THE EXEMPLARY CHOICE WHICH TOOK PLACE AT THE BEGINNING OF THE WORLD

('Gāthā:Yasna' 30)

Yasna 30 is one of the clearest and most frequently quoted Gāthās.
Zarathustra manifests his powerful originality by reducing the history
of the origins to that of a choice. . . . Better still, in Zoroaster's poem
this tale of the original choice is balanced by an announcement of the
final things, choice and rewards being closely interdependent. The
whole human drama, reduced to its essential structure, is contained in
a few stanzas.

1. Now will I speak to those who will hear
   Of the things which the initiate should remember;
   The praises and prayer of the Good Mind to the Lord
   And the joy which he shall see in the light who has remembered
     them well.

2. Hear with your ears that which is the sovereign good;
   With a clear mind look upon the two sides
   Between which each man must choose for himself,
   Watchful beforehand that the great test may be accomplished in
     our favour.

3. Now at the beginning the twin spirits have declared their nature,
   The better and the evil,
   In thought and word and deed. And between the two
   The wise ones choose well, not so the foolish.

4. And when these two spirits came together,
   In the beginning they established life and non-life,

And that at the last the worst experience should be for the wicked,
But for the righteous one the Best Mind.

5. Of these two spirits, the evil one chose to do the worst things;
But the most Holy Spirit, clothed in the most steadfast heavens,
Joined himself unto Righteousness;
And thus did all those who delight to please the Wise Lord by
honest deeds.

6. Between the two, the false gods also did not choose rightly,
For while they pondered they were beset by error,
So that they chose the Worst Mind.
Then did they hasten to join themselves unto Fury,
That they might by it deprave the existence of man.

7. And to him came Devotion, together with Dominion, Good Mind
and Righteousness;
She gave perpetuity of body and the breath of life,
That he may be thine apart from them,
As the first by the retributions through the metal.

8. And when their punishment shall come to these sinners,
Then, O Wise One, shall thy Dominion, with the Good Mind,
Be granted to those who have delivered Evil into the hands of
Righteousness, O Lord!

9. And may we be those that renew this existence!
O Wise One, and you other Lords, and Righteousness, bring
your alliance,
That thoughts may gather where wisdom is faint.

10. Then shall Evil cease to flourish,
While those who have acquired good fame
Shall reap the promised reward
In the blessed dwelling of the Good Mind, of the Wise One, and of
Righteousness.

11. If you, O men, understand the commandments which the Wise
One has given,
Well-being and suffering—long torment for the wicked and
salvation for the righteous—
All shall hereafter be for the best.

Translation and introductory note by Jacques
Duchesne-Guillemin, in his The Hymns of Zarathustra
(London, 1952), pp. 102-7

39. THE SECOND GĀTHĀ OF THE CHOICE

('Gāthā:Yasna' 31)

Yasna 31 is closely connected with the preceding one, Yasna 30. It adds supplementary words which are meant for the faithful and which were judged necessary because the choice to be made did not yet appear clearly enough.

7. He who first through the mind filled the blessed spaces with light,
   He it is who by his will created Righteousness,
   Whereby he upholds the Best Mind.
   This thou hast increased, O Wise One, by the Spirit
   Which is even now one with thee, O Lord!

8. Through the mind, O Wise One, have I known thee as the first
   and the last,
   As the father of the Good Mind,
   When I perceived thee with mine eyes as the true creator of
   Righteousness,
   As the Lord in the deeds of existence. . . .

11. Since thou, O Wise One, at the first didst create for us by thy mind
    Beings and consciences and wills,
    Since thou didst give a body to the soul of life,
    Since thou didst create deeds and words, that man may decide freely,

12. Since then does the man of false words lift up his voice as well
    as the man of true words,
    The initiate as well as the non-initiate, each according to his heart
    and his mind.
    May devotion put to the proof, one after the other, the spirits
    where there is bewilderment!. . .

17. Is it righteous, or is it the wicked one that takes to himself the
    greater part?
    Let him that knows speak knowledge; let the unlearned cease to
    deceive!
    O wise Lord, be thou our teacher in Good Mind! . . .

20. Whoever stands by the righteous man, to him shall future glory
    appear,

72

Long-lasting darkness, ill food, and wailing—
To such an existence shall your conscience
Lead you by your own deeds, O wicked ones.

Translation and introductory note by Jacques
Duchesne-Guillemin, in his *The Hymns of Zarathustra*
(London, 1952), pp. 108-17

D. ISLAM: ALLAH AND HIS PROPHET

40. MUHAMMAD SPEAKS OF ALLAH: 'THERE IS NO GOD BUT HE . . .'

('Koran,' II, 256-9; VI, 102-3)

God
there is no god but He, the
Living, the Everlasting.
Slumber seizes Him not, neither sleep;
    to Him belongs
all that is in the heavens and the earth
Who is there that shall intercede with Him
    save by His leave?
He knows what lies before them
    and what is after them,
and they comprehend not anything of His knowledge
    save such as He wills.
His Throne comprises the heavens and earth;
    the preserving of them oppresses Him not;
He is the All-high, the All-glorious.

No compulsion is there in religion.
Rectitude has become clear from error.
So whosoever disbelieves in idols
and believes in God, has laid hold of
the most firm handle, unbreaking; God is
    All-hearing, All-knowing.
God is the protector of the believers;
He brings them forth from the shadows
    into the light.
And the unbelievers—their protectors are
idols, that bring them forth from the light
    into the shadows;
those are the inhabitants of the Fire,
    therein dwelling forever. (II, 256-9)

That then is God your Lord;
there is no god but He,
the Creator of everything.
So serve Him,
for He is Guardian over everything.
The eyes attain Him not, but He attains the eyes;
He is the All-subtle, the All-aware. (VI, 102-3.)

Translation by A. J. Arberry

41. ALLAH IS ALL-KNOWING, ALL-POWERFUL—
THE CREATOR!

('Koran,' XXVII, 61-5; XXX, 47-54; XXXV, 36-9)

He who created the heavens and earth, and sent down for you
    out of heaven water;
and We caused to grow therewith gardens full of loveliness
    whose trees you could never grow.
        Is there a god with God?
Nay, but they are a people who assign to Him equals!

He who made the earth a fixed place
    and set amidst it rivers
and appointed it firm mountains
and placed a partition between the two seas.
        Is there a god with God?
Nay, but the most of them have no knowledge.

He who answers the constrained, when he calls unto Him,
    and removes the evil
and appoints you to be successors in the earth.
        Is there a god with God?
    Little indeed do you remember.

He who guides you in the shadows of the land and the sea
    and looses the winds,
    bearing good tidings before His mercy.
        Is there a god with God?
High exalted be God, above that which they associate!

Who originates creation, then brings it back again,
   and provides you out of heaven and earth.
         Is there a god with God? (XXVII, 61-5.)

God is He that looses the winds, that stirs up clouds,
and He spreads them in heaven how He will, and shatters them;
then thou seest the rain issuing out of the midst of them,
and when he smites with it whomsoever of His servants
         He will, lo, they rejoice,
although before it was sent down on them before that
      they had been in despair.

    So behold the marks of God's mercy,
    how He quickens the earth after it
    was dead; surely He is the quickener
    of the dead, and He is powerful
    over everything.
But if We loose a wind, and they see it growing yellow,
    they remain after that unbelievers.

    Thou shalt not make the dead to hear,
   neither shalt thou make the deaf to hear the call
    when they turn about, retreating.
   Thou shalt not guide the blind out of their error
    neither shalt thou make any to hear
except for such as believe in Our signs, and so surrender.

God is He that created you of weakness, then He appointed
after weakness strength, then after strength He appointed
weakness and grey hairs; He creates what He will, and
    He is the All-knowing, the All-powerful. (XXX, 47-54.)

God knows the Unseen in the heavens and the earth;
   He knows the thoughts within the breasts.
It is He who appointed you viceroys in the earth.
So whosoever disbelieves, his unbelief shall be
charged against him; their unbelief increases
the disbelievers only in hate in God's sight;
their unbelief increases the disbelievers only in loss.
Say: 'Have you considered your associates on whom
you call, apart from God? Show what they have
created in the earth; or have they a partnership
in the heavens?' Or have We given them a Book,
so that they are upon a clear sign from it?

Nay, but the evildoers promise one another
   naught but delusion.

God holds the heavens and the earth, lest they remove;
did they remove, none would hold them after Him
   Surely He is All-clement, All-forgiving. (XXXV, 36-9.)

Translation by A. J. Arberry

42. ALLAH 'IS THE FIRST AND THE LAST,' THE CREATOR,
MAKER, AND SHAPER ... HE HAS KNOWLEDGE OF
EVERYTHING

('Koran,' LVII, 1-5; LVIII, 7-8; LIX, 23-5)

In the Name of God, the Merciful, the Compassionate

All that is in the heavens and the earth magnifies God;
   He is the All-mighty, the All-wise.
To Him belongs the Kingdom of the heavens and the earth;
He gives life, and He makes to die, and He is powerful
   Over everything.
He is the First and the Last, the Outward and the Inward;
   He has knowledge of everything.
   It is He that created the heavens and the earth
   in six days
   then seated Himself upon the Throne.
   He knows what penetrates into the earth
   and what comes forth from it,
what comes down from heaven, and what goes up into it.
   He is with you wherever you are; and God sees
   the things you do.
To Him belongs the Kingdom of the heavens and the earth;
   and unto Him all matters are returned,
   He makes the night to enter into the day
   and makes the day to enter into the night.
   He knows the thoughts within the breasts. (LVII, 1-5.)

Hast thou not seen that God knows whatsoever is in
the heavens, and whatsoever is in the earth? Three

men conspire not secretly together, but He is the
fourth of them, neither five men, but He is the
sixth of them, neither fewer than that, neither
more, but He is with them, wherever they may be;
then He shall tell them what they have done, on the
Day of Resurrection. Surely God has knowledge
of everything. (LIV, 7-8.)

> He is God;
> There is no god but He.
> He is the knower of the Unseen and the Visible;
> He is the All-merciful, the All-compassionate.

> He is God;
> There is no god but He.
> He is the King, the All-holy, the All-peaceable,
> the All-faithful, the All-preserver,
> the All-mighty, the All-compeller,
> the All-sublime.
> Glory be to God, above that they associate!

> He is God;
> the Creator, the Maker, the Shaper.
> To Him belong the Names Most Beautiful.
> All that is in the heavens and the earth magnifies Him;
> He is the All-mighty, the All-wise. (LIX, 23-5.)

Translation by A. J. Arberry

43. ALLAH IS LIGHT . . .

('Koran,' XXIV, 33-44)

Now We have sent down to you signs
making all clear, and an example
of those who passed away before you,
and an admonition for the godfearing.

God is the Light of the heavens and the earth;
the likeness of His Light is as a niche
wherein is a lamp
(the lamp is a glass,

the glass as it were a glittering star)
    kindled from a Blessed Tree,
  an olive that is neither of the East nor of the West
whose oil wellnigh would shine, even if no fire touched it;
    Light upon Light;
  (God guides to His Light whom He will.)
  (And God strikes similitudes for men,
  and God has knowledge of everything.)
  in temples God has allowed to be raised up,
  and His name to be commemorated therein;
therein glorifying Him, in the mornings and the evenings,
  are men whom neither commerce nor trafficking
    diverts from the remembrance of God
  and to perform the prayer, and to pay the alms,
fearing a day when hearts and eyes shall be turned about,
that God may recompense them for their fairest works
    and give them increase of His bounty;
and God provides whomsoever He will, without reckoning.
    And as for the unbelievers,
their works are as a mirage in a spacious plain
  which the man athirst supposes to be water
    till, when he comes to it, he finds it is nothing;
    there indeed he finds God,
and He pays him his account in full; (And God is swift
    at the reckoning.)
  or they are as shadows upon a sea obscure
    covered by a billow
    above which is a billow
    above which are clouds,
    shadows piled one upon another;
when he puts forth his hand, wellnigh he cannot see it.
  And to whomsoever God assigns no light,
-    no light has he.
Hast thou not seen how that whatsoever is in the heavens
    and in the earth extols God,
    and the birds spreading their wings?
Each—He knows its prayer and its extolling; and God knows
    the things they do.
To God belongs the Kingdom of the heavens and the earth,
    and to Him is the homecoming.
Hast thou not seen how God drives the clouds, then composes them,

then converts them into a mass,
then thou seest the rain issuing out of the midst of them?
And He sends down out of heaven mountains, wherein is hail,
so that He smites whom He will with it, and turns it aside
from whom He will;
wellnigh the gleam of His lightning snatches away at the sight.
God turns about the day and the night;
surely in that is a lesson for those who have eyes.
God has created every beast of water,
And some of them go upon their bellies,
and some of them go upon two feet,
and some of them go upon four; God
creates whatever He will; God is powerful
over everything.

Translation by A. J. Arberry

See also nos. 231-7, 252, 268-9

CHAPTER II

Myths of Creation
and of Origin

A. MYTHS OF THE CREATION OF THE WORLD

There is a great variety of cosmogonic myths. However, they can be classified as follows: 1. creation ex nihilo (a High Being creates the world by thought, by word, or by heating himself in a steam-hut, and so forth); 2. The Earth Diver Motif (a God sends aquatic birds or amphibious animals, or dives, himself, to the bottom of the primordial ocean to bring up a particle of earth from which the entire world grows); 3. creation by dividing in two a primordial unity (one can distinguish three variants: a. separation of Heaven and Earth, that is to say of the World-Parents; b. separation of an original amorphous mass, the 'Chaos'; c. the cutting in two of a cosmogenic egg); 4. creation by dismemberment of a primordial Being, either a voluntary, anthropomorphic victim (Ymir of the Scandinavian mythology, the Vedic Indian Purusha, the Chinese P'an-ku) or an aquatic monster conquered after a terrific battle (the Babylonian Tiamat). The texts reprinted below cover almost all of these types and variants. We have added some examples of Indian speculative cosmogonic texts.

44. CREATION BY THOUGHT

An account by a Winnebago Indian of Wisconsin, recorded by Paul Radin.

'What it was our father lay on when he came to consciousness we do not know. He moved his right arm and then his left arm, his right leg and then his left leg. He began to think of what he should do and finally be began to cry and tears began to flow from his eyes and fall down below him. After a while he looked down below him and saw something bright. The bright objects were his tears that had flowed below and formed the present waters. . . . Earthmaker began to think again. He thought: "It is thus, If I wish anything it will become as I wish, just as my tears have become seas." Thus he thought. So he wished for light and it became light. Then he thought: "It is as I supposed; the things that I have wished for have come into existence as I desired." Then he again thought and wished for the earth and this earth came into existence. Earthmaker looked at the earth and he liked it but it was not quiet. . . . (After the earth had become quiet) he thought again of how things came into existence just as he desired. Then he first began to talk. He said, "As things are just as I wish them I shall make one being like myself." So he took a piece of earth and made it like himself. Then he talked to what he had created but it did not answer. He looked upon it and he saw that it had no mind or thought. So he made a mind for it. Again he talked to it, but it did not answer. So he looked upon it again and saw that it had no tongue. Then he made it a tongue. Then he talked to it again but it did not answer. So he looked upon it again and saw that it had no soul. So he made it a soul. He talked to it again and it very nearly said something. But it did not make itself intelligible. So Earthmaker breathed into its mouth and talked to it and it answered.'

Paul Radin, 'The Winnebago Indians,' in *Thirty-seventh Annual Report*, Bureau of American Ethnology (Washington, D.C., 1923), pp. 212-13

45. OMAHA COSMOGONY: AT THE BEGINNING THE WORLD WAS IN GOD'S MIND

An Omaha Indian explains the Omaha belief about the creation of the world as recorded by Fletcher and La Flesche.

'At the beginning,' said the Omaha, 'all things were in the mind of Wakonda. All creatures, including man, were spirits. They moved about in space between the earth and the stars (the heavens). They were seeking a place where they could come into bodily existence. They ascended to the sun, but the sun was not fitted for their abode. They moved on to the moon and found that it also was not good for their home. Then they descended to the earth. They saw it was covered with water. They floated through the air to the north, the east, the south, and the west, and found no dry land. They were sorely grieved. Suddenly from the midst of the water uprose a great rock. It burst into flames and the waters floated into the air in clouds. Dry land appeared; the grasses and the trees grew. The hosts of the spirits descended and became flesh and blood. They fed on the seeds of the grasses and the fruits of the trees, and the land vibrated with their expressions of joy and gratitude to Wakonda, the maker of all things.'

Fletcher and La Flesche, 'The Omaha Tribe,' in *Twenty-seventh Annual Report*, Bureau of American Ethnology, (Washington, D.C., 1911), pp. 570-1.

See also nos. 8, 9, 10

46. CREATION FROM MERE APPEARANCE

A belief of the Uitoto of Colombia, South America.

In the beginning there was nothing but mere appearance, nothing really existed. It was a phantasm, an illusion that our father touched; something mysterious it was that he grasped. Nothing existed. Through the agency of a dream our father, He-who-is-appearance-only, Nainema, pressed the phantasm to his breast and then was sunk in thought.

Not even a tree existed that might have supported this phantasm and only through his breath did Nainema hold this illusion attached to the thread of a dream. He tried to discover what was at the bottom of it, but he found nothing. 'I have attached that which was non-existent,' he said. There was nothing.

Then our father tried again and investigated the bottom of this something and his fingers sought the empty phantasm. He tied the emptiness to the dream-thread and pressed the magical glue-substance upon it. Thus by means of his dream did he hold it like the fluff of raw cotton.

He seized the bottom of the phantasm and stamped upon it repeatedly, allowing himself finally to rest upon the earth of which he had dreamt.

The earth-phantasm was now his. Then he spat out saliva repeatedly so that the forests might arise. He lay upon the earth and set the covering of heaven above it. He drew from the earth the blue and white heavens and placed them above.

Paul Radin, *Monotheism among Primitive Peoples* (Basel, 1954), pp. 13-14; paraphrasing and summarizing K. T. Preuss, *Religion und Mythologie der Uitoto*, I (Göttingen, 1921), pp. 166-8

47. IO AND THE MAORI COSMOGONY

Io (Iho), the Supreme Being of the Maori of New Zealand, is regarded
as eternal, omniscient, and the creator of the universe, of the gods, and
of man. As will be seen from the following text, the cosmogonic myth
constitutes, for the Maori, a paradigmatic model for every kind of
'creation': the procreation of a child, the inspiration of a poet, and the
like. (Cf. M. Eliade, 'Myth and Reality' [New York: Harper & Row,
1963], pp. 30 ff.)

Io dwelt within the breathing-space of immensity.
The Universe was in darkness, with water everywhere.
There was no glimmer of dawn, no clearness, no light.
And he began by saying these words,—
That He might cease remaining inactive:
  'Darkness become a light-possessing darkness.'
And at once light appeared.
(He) then repeated those self-same words in this manner.
That He might cease remaining inactive:
  'Light, become a darkness-possessing light.'
And again an intense darkness supervened.
Then a third time He spake saying:
  'Let there be one darkness above,
  Let there be one darkness below.
  ....
  Let there be one light above,
  Let there be one light below,
  ....
  A dominion of light,
  A bright light.'
And now a great light prevailed.
(Io) then looked to the waters which compassed him about,
      and spake a fourth time, saying:
  'Ye waters of Tai-kama, be ye separate.
  Heaven, be formed.' Then the sky became suspended.
  'Bring forth thou Tupua-horo-nuku.'
And at once the moving earth lay stretched abroad.

Those words (of Io) (the supreme god) became impressed on the minds
of our ancestors, and by them were they transmitted down through
generations, our priest joyously referred to them as being:

The Creation of the World

The ancient and original sayings.
The ancient and original words.
The ancient and original cosmological wisdom (wananga).
Which caused growth from the void,
The limitless space-filling void,
As witness the tidal-waters,
The evolved heaven,
The birth-given evolved earth.

And now, my friends, there are three very important applications of those original sayings, as used in our sacred rituals. The first occurs in the ritual for planting a child in the barren womb.

The next occurs in the ritual for enlightening both the mind and body. The third and last occurs in the ritual on the solemn subject of death, and of war, of baptism, of genealogical recitals and such like important subjects, as the priests most particularly concerned themselves in.

The words by which Io fashioned the Universe—that is to say, by which it was implanted and caused to produce a world of light—the same words are used in the ritual for implanting a child in a barren womb. The words by which Io caused light to shine in the darkness are used in the rituals for cheering a gloomy and despondent heart, the feeble aged, the decrepit; for shedding light into secret places and matters, for inspiration in song-composing, and in many other affairs, affecting man to despair in times of adverse war. For all such the ritual to enlighten and cheer includes the words (used by Io) to overcome and dispel darkness. Thirdly, there is the preparatory ritual which treats of successive formations within the universe, and the genealogical history of man himself.

Hare Hongi, 'A Maori Cosmogony,' *Journal of the Polynesian Society*, XVI (1907), pp. 113-14

See also no. 11

48. POLYNESIAN THEOGONY AND COSMOGONY
(SOCIETY ISLANDS)

Ta'aroa (Tangararoa) is the Supreme Being, the noncreated Creator of the universe. He came forth from a shell (Rumia), which later became the world.

Ta'aroa was the ancestor of all the gods; he made everything. From time immemorial was the great Ta'aroa, Tahi-tumu (The-origin). Ta'aroa developed himself in solitude; he was his own parent, having no father or mother. . . .

Ta'aroa sat in his shell in darkness from eternity. The shell was like an egg revolving in endless space, with no sky, no land, no sea, no moon, no sun, no stars. All was darkness, it was continuous thick darkness. . . . The record then proceeds to describe Ta'aroa's breaking his shell, which became the sky, his swimming in empty space and retirement into a new shell which, after he had again emerged, . . . he took . . . for the great foundation of the world, for stratum rock and for soil for the world.

And the shell Rumia that he opened first, became his house, the dome of the gods' sky, which was a confined sky, enclosing the world then forming.

E. S. Craighill Handy, *Polynesian Religion*, Bernice P. Bishop Museum Bulletin 34 (Honolulu, 1927), pp. 11-12

49. AN EARTH-DIVER CREATION MYTH

Beliefs of the Maidu Indians of California.

In the beginning there was no sun, no moon, no stars. All was dark, and everywhere there was only water. A raft came floating on the water. It came from the north, and in it were two persons,—Turtle (A'nōshma) and Father-of-the-Secret-Society (Pehē'ipe). The stream flowed very rapidly. Then from the sky a rope of feathers, called Pō'kelma, was let down, and down it came Earth-Initiate. When he reached the end of the rope, he tied it to the bow of the raft, and stepped in. His face was covered and was never seen, but his body shone like the sun. He sat down, and for a long time said nothing. At last Turtle said, 'Where do you come from?' and Earth-Initiate answered, 'I come from above.' Then Turtle said, 'Brother, can you not make for me some good dry land, so that I may sometimes come up out of the water?' Then he asked another time, 'Are there going to be any people in the world?' Earth-Initiate thought awhile, then said, 'Yes.' Turtle asked, 'How long before you are going to make people?' Earth-Initiate replied, 'I don't know. You want to have some dry land: well, how am I going to get any earth to make it of?' Turtle answered, 'If you will tie a rock about my left arm, I'll dive for some.' Earth-Initiate did as Turtle asked, and then, reaching around, took the end of a rope from somewhere, and tied it to Turtle. When Earth-Initiate came to the raft, there was no rope there: he just reached out and found one. Turtle said, 'If the rope is not long enough, I'll jerk it once, and you must haul me up; if it is long enough, I'll give two jerks, and then you must pull me up quickly, as I shall have all the earth that I can carry.' Just as Turtle went over the side of the boat, Father-of-the-Secret-Society began to shout loudly.

Turtle was gone a long time. He was gone six years; and when he came up, he was covered with green slime, he had been down so long. When he reached the top of the water, the only earth he had was a very little under his nails; the rest had all washed away. Earth-Initiate took with his right hand a stone knife from under his left armpit, and carefully scraped the earth out from under Turtle's nails. He put the earth in the palm of his hand, and rolled it about till it was round; it was as large as a small pebble. He laid it on the stern of the raft. By and by he went to look at it; it had not grown at all. The third time he went to look at it, it had grown so that it could be spanned by the arms. The fourth time he looked, it was as big as the world, the raft was aground, and all around were mountains as far as he could see. The raft came ashore at Tadoikō and the place can be seen today.

When the raft had come to land, Turtle said, 'I can't stay in the dark all the time. Can't you make a light, so that I can see?' Earth-Initiate replied, 'Let us get out of the raft, and then we will see what we can do.' So all three got out. Then, Earth-Initiate said, 'Look that way, to the east! I am going to tell my sister to come up. Then it began to grow light, and day began to break; then Father-of-the-Secret-Society began to shout loudly, and the sun came up. Turtle said 'Which way is the sun going to travel?' Earth-Initiate answered, 'I'll tell her to go this way, and go down there.' After the sun went down, Father-of-the-Secret-Society began to cry and shout again, and it grew very dark. Earth-Initiate asked Turtle and Father-of-the-Secret-Society, 'How do you like it?' and they both answered, 'It is very good.' Then Turtle asked, 'Is that all you are going to do for us?' and Earth-Initiate answered, 'No, I am going to do more yet.' Then he called the stars each by its name, and they came out. When this was done,

Turtle asked, 'Now what shall we do?' Earth-Initiate replied, 'Wait, and I'll show you.' Then he made a tree grow at Ta'doikö,—the tree called Hu'kimsta and Earth-Initiate and Turtle and Father-of-the-Secret-Society sat in its shade for two days. The tree was very large, and had twelve different kinds of acorns growing on it.

Roland B. Dixon, *Maidu Myths*, Bulletin of the American Museum of Natural History, XVII, no. 2 (1902-7) pp. 33-118; quotation from pp. 39 *ff*.

50. THE BEGINNING OF THE WORLD

A myth from the Yauelmani Yokuts of California.

At first there was water everywhere. A piece of wood (wicket, stick, wood, tree) grew up out of the water to the sky. On the tree there was a nest. Those who were inside did not see any earth. There was only water to be seen. The eagle was the chief of them. With him were the wolf, Coyote, the panther, the prairie falcon, the hawk called *po'yon*, and the condor. The eagle wanted to make the earth. He thought, 'We will have to have land.' Then he called *k'uik'ui*, a small duck. He said to it: 'Dive down and bring up earth.' The duck dived, but did not reach the bottom. It died. The eagle called another kind of duck. He told it to dive. This duck went far down. It finally reached the bottom. Just as it touched the mud there it died. Then it came up again. Then the eagle and the other six saw a little dirt under its finger nail. When the eagle saw this he took the dirt from its nail. He mixed it with *telis* and *pele* seeds and ground them up. He put water with the mixture and made dough. This was in the morning. Then he set it in the water and it swelled and spread everywhere, going out from the middle. (These seeds when ground and mixed with water swell.) In the evening the eagle told his companions: 'Take some earth.' They went down and took a little earth up in the tree with them. Early in the morning, when the morning star came, the eagle said to the wolf: 'Shout.' The wolf shouted and the earth disappeared, and all was water again. The eagle said: 'We will make it again,' for it was for this purpose that they had taken some earth with them into the nest. Then they took *telis* and *pele* seeds again, and ground them with the earth, and put the mixture into the water, and it swelled out again. Then early next morning, when the morning star appeared, the eagle told the wolf again: 'Shout!' and he shouted three times. The earth was shaken by the earthquake, but it stood. Then Coyote said: 'I must shout too.' He shouted and the earth shook a very little. Now it was good. Then they came out of the tree on the ground. Close to where this tree stood there was a lake. The eagle said: 'We will live here.' Then they had a house there and lived there.

A. L. Kroeber, *Indian Myths of South Central California*, University of California Publications, American Archeology and Ethnology, IV, no. 4 (1906-7), pp. 229-31

51. AN AFRICAN COSMOGONY

An account from the Boshongo, a Central Bantu Tribe of the Lunda Cluster

In the beginning, in the dark, there was nothing but water. And Bumba was alone.

One day Bumba was in terrible pain. He retched and strained and vomited up the sun. After that light spread over everything. The heat of the sun dried up the water until the black edges of the world began to show. Black sandbanks and reefs could be seen. But there were no living things.

Bumba vomited up the moon and then the stars, and after that the night had its light also.

Still Bumba was in pain. He strained again and nine living creatures came forth; the leopard named Koy Bumba, and Pongo Bumba the crested eagle, the crocodile, Ganda Bumba, and one little fish named Yo; next, old Kono Bumba, the tortoise, and Tsetse, the lightning, swift, deadly, beautiful like the leopard, then the white heron, Nyanyi Bumba, also one beetle, and the goat named Budi.

Last of all came forth men. There were many men, but only one was white like Bumba. His name was Loko Yima.

The creatures themselves then created all the creatures. The heron created all the birds of the air except the kite. He did not make the kite. The crocodile made serpents and the iguana. The goat produced every beast with horns. Yo, the small fish, brought forth all the fish of all the seas and waters. The beetle created insects.

Then the serpents in their turn made grasshoppers, and the iguana made the creatures without horns.

Then the three sons of Bumba said they would finish the world. The first, Nyonye Ngana, made the white ants; but he was not equal to the task, and died of it. The ants, however, thankful for life and being, went searching for black earth in the depths of the world and covered the barren sands to bury and honour their creator.

Chonganda, the second son, brought forth a marvellous living plant from which all the trees and grasses and flowers and plants in the world have sprung. The third son, Chedi Bumba, wanted something different, but for all his trying made only the bird called the kite.

Of all the creatures, Tsetse, lightning, was the only trouble-maker. She stirred up so much trouble that Bumba chased her into the sky. Then mankind was without fire until Bumba showed the people how to draw fire out of trees. 'There is fire in every tree,' he told them, and showed them how to make the firedrill and liberate it. Sometimes today Tsetse still leaps down and strikes the earth and causes damage.

When at last the work of creation was finished, Bumba walked through the peaceful villages and said to the people, 'Behold these wonders. They belong to you.' Thus from Bumba, the Creator, the First Ancestor, came forth all the wonders that we see and hold and use, and all the brotherhood of beasts and man.

Maria Leach, *The Beginning* (New York, 1956), pp. 145-6; translated and adapted from E. Torday and J. A. Joyce, *Les Boshongo*, pp. 20 *f*.

52. THE MAYA-QUICHÉ GENESIS

('Popol Vuh,' chapter 1)

The 'Popol Vuh' is the most important surviving work of Mayan literature. It was first written down after the introduction of Christianity.

Admirable is the account—so the narrative opens—admirable is the account of the time in which it came to pass that all was formed in heaven and upon earth, the quartering of their signs, their measure and alignment, and the establishment of parallels to the skies and upon the earth to the four quarters thereof, as was spoken by the Creator and Maker, the Mother, the Father of life and of all existence, that one by whom all move and breathe, father and sustainer of the peace of peoples, by whose wisdom was premediated the excellence of all that doth exist in the heavens, upon the earth, in lake and sea.

Lo, all was in suspense, all was calm and silent; all was motionless, all was quiet, and wide was the immensity of the skies.

Lo, the first word and the first discourse. There was not yet a man, not an animal; there were no birds nor fish nor crayfish; there was no wood, no stone, no bog, no ravine, neither vegetation nor marsh; only the sky existed.

The face of the earth was not yet to be seen; only the peaceful sea and the expanse of the heavens.

Nothing was yet formed into a body; nothing was joined to another thing; naught held itself poised; there was not a rustle, not a sound beneath the sky. There was naught that stood upright; there were only the quiet waters of the sea, solitary within its bounds; for as yet naught existed.

There were only immobility and silence in the darkness and in the night. Alone was the Creator, the Maker, Tepeu, the Lord, and Gucumatz, the Plumed Serpent, those who engender, those who give being, alone upon the waters like a growing light.

They are enveloped in green and azure, whence is the name Gucumatz, and their being is great wisdom. Lo, how the sky existeth, how the Heart of the Sky existeth—for such is the name of God, as He doth name Himself!

It is then that the word came to Tepeu and to Gucumatz, in the shadows and in the night, and spake with Tepeu and with Gucumatz. And they spake and consulted and meditated, and they joined their words and their counsels.

Then light came while they consulted together; and at the moment of dawn man appeared while they planned concerning the production and increase of the groves and of the climbing vines, there in the shade and in the night, through that one who is the Heart of the Sky, whose name is Hurakan.

The Lightning is the first sign of Hurakan; the second is the Streak of Lightning; the third is the Thunderbolt which striketh; and these three are the Heart of the Sky.

Then they came to Tepeu, the Gucumatz, and held counsel touching civilized life; how seed should be formed, how light should be produced, how the sustainer and nourisher of all.

'Let it be thus done. Let the waters retire and cease to obstruct, to

the end that earth exist here, that it harden itself and show its surface, to the end that it be sown, and that the light of day shine in
the heavens and upon the earth; for we shall receive neither glory nor
honour from all that we have created and formed until human beings
exist, endowed with sentience.' Thus they spake while the earth was
formed by them. It is thus, veritably, that creation took place, and the
earth existed. 'Earth,' they said, and immediately it was formed.

Like a fog or a cloud was its formation into the material state,
when, like great lobsters, the mountains appeared upon the waters,
and in an instant there were great mountains. Only by marvellous
power could have been achieved this their resolution when the mountains and the valleys instantly appeared, with groves of cypress and
pine upon them.

Then was Gucumatz filled with joy. 'Thou art welcome, O Heart of
the Sky, O Hurakan, O Streak of Lightning, O Thunderbolt!'

'This that we have created and shaped will have its end,' they replied.

Translation by H. B. Alexander in his *Latin-American
Mythology* (Boston, 1920), pp. 160-2

53. JAPANESE COSMOGONY

('Nihongi' and 'Ko-ji-ki')

At the beginning of the eighth century A.D., *the early Japanese myths
were gathered together in two collections: 'Nihongi' ('Chronicles of
Japan') and 'Ko-ji-ki' ('Records of Ancient Matters').*

Of old, Heaven and Earth were not yet separated, and the In and Yo
not yet divided. They formed a chaotic mass like an egg, which was of
obscurely defined limits, and contained germs. The purer and clearer
part was thinly diffused and formed Heaven, while the heavier and
grosser element settled down and became Earth. The finer element
easily became a united body, but the consolidation of the heavy and
gross element was accomplished with difficulty. Heaven was therefore
formed first, and Earth established subsequently. Thereafter divine
beings were produced between them. (*Nihongi*, pp. 1-2.)

We have next what is called 'the seven generations of Gods,' ending

The Creation of the World

with the creator-deities, Izanagi, the Male-Who-Invites, and his sister, Izanami, the Female-Who-Invites.

Hereupon all the Heavenly Deities commanded the two Deities His Augustness the Male-Who-Invites and Her Augustness the Female-Who-Invites, ordering them to 'Make, consolidate and give birth to this drifting land.' Granting to them an heavenly jewelled spear, they (thus) deigned to charge them. So the two Deities, standing upon the Floating Bridge of Heaven, pushed down the jewelled spear and stirred with it, whereupon, when they had stirred the brine till it went curdlecurdle, and drew (the spear) up, the brine that dripped down from the end of the spear was piled up and became an island. This is the Island of Onogoro. (*Ko-ji-ki*, p. 19.)

The two Deities having descended on Onogoro-jima erected there an eight fathom house with an august central pillar. Then Izanagi addressed Izanami, saying: 'How is thy body formed?' Izanami replied, 'My body is completely formed except one part which is incomplete.' Then Izanagi said, 'My body is completely formed and there is one part which is superfluous. Suppose that we supplement that which is incomplete in thee with that which is superfluous in me, and thereby procreate lands.' Izanami replied, 'It is well.' Then Izanagi said, 'Let me and thee go round the heavenly august pillar, and having met at the other side, let us become united in wedlock.' This being agreed to, he said, 'Do thou go round from the left, and I will go round from the right.' When they had gone round, Izanami spoke and exclaimed, 'How delightful! I have met a lovely youth.' Izanagi then said, 'How delightful! I have met a lovely maiden.' Afterwards he said, 'It was unlucky for the woman to speak first.' The child which was the first offspring of their union was the Hiruko (leech-child), which at the age of three was still unable to stand upright, and was therefore placed in a reed-boat and sent adrift. (*Nihongi*, p. 13; cf. *Ko-ji-ki*, pp. 20-1.)

The two deities next give birth to the islands of Japan and a number of deities. The last deity to be produced is the God of Fire. But in giving birth to him Izanami is mortally burned. After death, she descends beneath the earth. Izanagi goes in search of her, like Orpheus descending into the Shades to recover Eurydice. Under the earth it is very dark; but Izanagi finally meets his wife and offers to bring her back with him. Izanami begs him to wait at the door of the subterranean palace, and not to show a light. But the husband loses patience; he lights a tooth of his comb and enters the palace where, by the flame of this torch, he perceives Izanami in process of decomposition; seized with panic, he flees. His dead wife pursues him but Izanagi, managing to escape by the same way that he had gone down under the earth, casts a great rock over the aperture. Husband and wife talk together for the last time, separated from each other by this rock. Izanagi pronounces the sacramental formula for separation between them, and then goes up to heaven; while Izanami goes down forever into subterranean regions. She becomes the Goddess of the dead, as is generally the case with chthonian and agricultural goddesses, who are divinities of fecundity and, at the same time, of death, of birth, and of re-entry into the maternal bosom.

Nihongi translated by W. G. Aston (London, 1924).
Ko-ji-ki translated by B. H. Chamberlain (Tokyo: Asiatic Society of Japan, 1906)

54. EGYPTIAN COSMOGONY AND THEOGONY

('The Book of Overthrowing Apophis')

The following text is from 'The Book of Overthrowing Apophis,' a late work, but one which conserves basic material from a relatively early period.

The Lord of All, after having come into being, says: I am he who came into being as Khepri (i.e., the Becoming One). When I came into being, the beings came into being, all the beings came into being after I became. Numerous are those who became, who came out of my mouth, before heaven ever existed, nor earth came into being, nor the worms, nor snakes were created in this place. I, being in weariness, was bound to them in the Watery Abyss. I found no place to stand. I thought in my heart, I planned in myself, I made all forms being alone, before I ejected Shu, before I spat out Tefnut,[1] before any other who was in me had become. Then I planned in my own heart, and many forms of beings came into being as forms of children, as forms of their children. I conceived by my hand, I united myself with my hand, I poured out of my own mouth. I ejected Shu, I spat out

Tefnut. It was my father the Watery Abyss who brought them up, and my eye followed them (?) while they became far from me. After having become one god, there were (now) three gods in me. When I came into being in this land, Shu and Tefnut jubilated in the Watery Abyss in which they were. Then they brought with them my eye. After I had joined together my members, I wept over them, and men came into being out of the tears which came out of my eyes.[2] Then she (the eye) became enraged[3] after she came back and had found that I had placed another in her place, that she had been replaced by the Brilliant One. Then I found a higher place for her on my brow,[4] and when she began to rule over the whole land her fury fell down on the flowering (?) and I replaced what she had ravished. I came out of the flowering (?), I created all snakes, and all that came into being with them. Shu and Tefnut produced Geb and Nut; Geb and Nut produced out of a single body Osiris, Horus the Eyeless One,[5] Seth, Isis, and Nephthys, one after the other among them. Their children are numerous in this land.

Notes

1 Shu the air, Tefnut the moist.
2 Same myth in the Book of Gates, division 4 (*The Tomb of Ramesses* VI, p. 169).
3 An allusion to the myth of the Eye of the sun god which departs into a foreign land and is brought back by Shu and Tefnut. Another aspect of this myth is to be found in the Book of the Divine Cow.
4 The fire-spitting snake, the uraeus on the head of the god.
5 The Elder Horus of Letopolis.

> Translation and notes by Alexandre Piankoff, in his *The Shrines of Tut-ankh-amon* (New York, 1955), p. 24. Cf. the translation by John A. Wilson, in ANET, pp. 6-7

See also no. 17

55. MESOPOTAMIAN COSMOGONY

('Enuma elish')

The long Babylonian creation epic 'Enuma elish' ('When on high'), so called from the first two words of the poem, narrates a chain of events beginning with the very first separation of order out of chaos and culminating in the creation of the specific cosmos known to the ancient Babylonians. As the gods are born within the commingled waters of their primeval parents, Apsu and Tiamat, their restlessness disturbs Apsu. Over Tiamat's protests, he plans to kill them; but the clever Ea learns of his plan and kills Apsu instead. Now Tiamat is furious; she produces an army of monsters to avenge her husband and to wrest lordship from the younger generation. The terrified gods turn to Ea's son Marduk for help. Marduk agrees to face Tiamat, but demands supremacy over them as compensation. They promptly assemble, declare him king, and send him forth, armed with his winds and storms. The battle is short; the winds inflate Tiamat's body like a balloon and Marduk sends an arrow through her gaping mouth into her heart. He then splits her body, forming heaven and earth with the two halves. After putting the heavens in order, he turns to Ea for help in creating, out of the blood of Tiamat's demon-commander Kingu, the black-haired men of Mesopotamia. The poem concludes as the gods build a temple for Marduk and gather in it to celebrate his mighty deeds. Enuma elish was probably composed in the early part of the second millennium B.C.

When on high the heaven had not been named,
Firm ground below had not been called by name,
Naught but primordial Apsu,[1] their begetter,
(And) Mummu[2]-Tiamat,[3] she who bore them all,
Their waters[4] commingling as a single body;
No reed hut had been matted, no marsh land had appeared,
When no gods whatever had been brought into being,
Uncalled by name, their destinies undetermined—
Then it was that the gods were formed within them.[5]
Lahmu and Lahamu[6] were brought forth, by name they were called.
For aeons they grew in age and stature.
Anshar and Kishar[7] were formed, surpassing the others.
They prolonged the days, added on the years.
Anu[8] was their son, of his fathers the rival;
Yea, Anshar's first-born, Anu, was his equal.
Anu begot in his image Nudimmud.[9]
This Nudimmud was of his fathers the master;
Of broad wisdom, understanding, mighty in strength,

The Creation of the World

Mightier by far than his grandfather, Anshar.
He had no rival among the gods, his brothers.
The divine brothers banded together,
They disturbed Tiamat as they surged back and forth,
Yea, they troubled the mood of Tiamat
By their hilarity in the Abode of Heaven.
Apsu could not lessen their clamour
And Tiamat was speechless at their ways.
Their doings were loathsome unto [. . .].
Unsavoury were their ways; they were overbearing.
Then Apsu, the begetter of the great gods,
Cried out, addressing Mummu, his vizier:
'O Mummu, my vizier, who rejoicest my spirit,
Come hither and let us go to Tiamat!'
They went and sat down before Tiamat,
Exchanging counsel about the gods, their first-born.
Apsu, opening his mouth,
Said unto resplendent Tiamat:
'Their ways are verily loathsome unto me.
By day I find no relief, nor repose by night.
I will destroy, I will wreck their ways,
That quiet may be restored. Let us have rest!'
As soon as Tiamat heard this,
She was wroth and called out to her husband.
She cried out aggrieved, as she raged all alone,
Injecting woe into her mood:
What? Should we destroy that which we have built?
Their ways are indeed troublesome, but let us attend kindly!'
Then answered Mummu, giving counsel to Apsu;
Ill-wishing and ungracious was Mummu's advice:
'Do destroy, my father, the mutinous ways.
Then shalt thou have relief by day and rest by night!'
When Apsu heard this, his face grew radiant
Because of the evil he planned against the gods, his sons.
As for Mummu, by the neck he embraced him
As (that one) sat down on his knees to kiss him.
(Now) whatever they had plotted between them
Was repeated unto the gods, their first born.
When the gods heard (this), they were astir,
(Then) lapsed into silence and remained speechless.
Surpassing in wisdom, accomplished, resourceful,

Ea,[10] the all-wise, saw through their[11] scheme.
A master design against it he devised and set up,
Made artful his spell against it, surpassing and holy.
He recited it and made is subsist in the deep,[12]
As he poured sleep upon him. Sound asleep he lay.
When Apsu he had made prone, drenched with sleep,
Mummu, the adviser, was impotent to move.
He loosened his band, tore off his tiara,
Removed his halo (and) put it on himself.
Having fettered Apsu, he slew him.
Mummu he bound and left behind lock.
Having thus upon Apsu established his dwelling,
He laid hold on Mummu, holding him by the nose-rope.
After he had vanquished and trodden down his foes,
Ea, his triumph over his enemies secured,
In his sacred chamber in profound peace he rested.
He named it 'Apsu,'[13] for shrines he assigned (it).
In that same place his cult hut he founded.
Ea and Damkina, his wife, dwelled (there) in splendour.
In the chamber of fates, the abode of destinies,
A god was engendered, most potent and wisest of gods.
In the heart of Apsu[14] was Marduk created,
In the heart of holy Apsu was Marduk created.
He who begot him was Ea, his father;
She who conceived him was Damkina, his mother.
The breast of goddessess did she suck.
The nurse that nursed him filled him with awsomeness.
Alluring was his figure, sparkling the lift in his eyes.
Lordly was his gait, commanding from of old.
When Ea saw him, the father who begot him,
He exulted and glowed, his heart filled with gladness.
He rendered him perfect and endowed him with a double godhead.
Greatly exalted was he above them, exceeding throughout.
Perfect were his members beyond comprehension,
Unsuited for understanding, difficult to perceive.
Four were his eyes, four were his ears;[15]
When he moved his lips, fire blazed forth.
Large were all hearing organs,
And the eyes, in like number, scanned all things.
He was the loftiest of the gods, surpassing was his stature;
His members were enormous, he was exceeding tall.

The Creation of the World

'My little son, my little son!'
My son, the Sun! Sun of the heavens!'
Clothed with the halo of ten gods, he was strong to the utmost,
As their awesome flashes were heaped upon him.

....

Disturbed was Tiamat, astir night and day.
The gods, in malice, contributed to the storm.
Their insides having plotted evil,
To Tiamat these brothers said:
'When they slew Apsu, thy consort,
Thou didst not aid him but remaindest still.
Although he fashioned the awesome Saw,[16]
Thy insides are diluted and so we can have no rest.
Let Apsu, thy consort, be in thy mind
And Mummu, who has been vanquished! Thou art left alone.

....

[Several of the preceding lines are fragmentary. The gods incite
Tiamat to avenge Apsu and Mummu. She is pleased and proposes to do
battle against the offending gods. But first she bears a horrible brood
of helpers—eleven monsters, 'Sharp of tooth, unsparing of fang/ With
venom for blood she has filled their bodies.']

From among the gods,[17] her first-born, who formed her Assembly,
She elevated Kingu, made him chief among them.
The leading of the ranks, command of the Assembly,
The raising weapons for the encounter, advancing to combat,
In battle the command-in-chief—
These to his hand she entrusted as she seated him in the Council:
'I have cast for thee the spell, exalting thee in the Assembly of the gods.
To counsel all the gods I have given thee full power.
Verily, thou art supreme, my only consort art thou!
Thy utterance shall prevail over all the Anunnaki!'[18]
She gave him the Tablets of Fate, fastened on his breast:
'As for thee, thy command shall be unchangeable, Thy word shall
     endure!'
As soon as Kingu was elevated, possessed of the rank of Anu,
For the gods, her sons, they[19] decreed the fate:
'Your word shall make the fire subside,
Shall humble the 'Power-Weapon,' so potent in (its) sweep!'

[Ea again learns of the plot; but this time he has no ready response

*for it. He goes to his grandfather Anshar and repeats the entire story
of Tiamat's fury and her preparations for battle. Anshar is profoundly
disturbed. Finally he dispatches Anu, saying, 'Go and stand thou up
to Tiamat,/ that her mood be calmed, that her heart expand.' But when
Anu sees the hosts of Tiamat, he loses his nerve and returns to Anshar.]*

He came abjectly to his father, Anshar.
As though he were Tiamat thus he addressed him:
'My hand suffices not for me to subdue thee.'
Speechless was Anshar as he stared at the ground,
Frowning and shaking his head at Ea.
All the Anunnaki gathered at that place;
Their lips closed tight, they sat in silence.
'No god' (thought they) 'can go to battle and,
Facing Tiamat, escape with his life.'
Lord Anshar, father of the gods, rose up in grandeur,
And having pondered in his heart, he said to the Anunnaki:
'He whose strength is potent shall be our avenger,
He who is keen in battle, Marduk, the hero!'

   *[Ea warns Marduk of Anshar's plan and advises him to go before
Anshar boldly. Marduk obeys and Anshar, seeing the hero, is instantly
calmed.]*

'Anshar, be not muted; open wide thy lips.
I will go and attain thy heart's desire. . . .
What male is it who has pressed his fight against thee?
It is but Tiamat, a woman, that opposes thee with weapons!
O my father-creator, be glad and rejoice;
The neck of Tiamat thou shalt soon tread upon!
. . . .
My son, (thou) who knowest all wisdom,
Calm Tiamat with thy holy spell.
On the storm-chariot proceed with all speed.
From her presence they shall not drive (thee)! Turn them back!'
The lord rejoiced at the word of his father.
His heart exulting, he said to his father:
'Creator of the gods, destiny of the great gods,
If I indeed, as your avenger,
Am to vanquish Tiamat and save your lives,
Set up the Assembly, proclaim supreme my destiny!
When jointly in Ubshukinna[20] you have sat down rejoicing,

Let my word, instead of you, determine the fates.
Unalterable shall be what I may bring into being;
Neither recalled nor changed shall be the command of my lips.'

[Anshar is prepared to accept Marduk's terms. He sends his vizier
Gaga to a still older generation of gods, Lahmu and Lahamu. Gaga is
instructed to repeat the entire story to them, and to invite the gods to
assemble at a banquet for fixing Marduk's decrees.]

When Lahmu and Lahamu heard this, they cried out aloud,
All the Igigi[21] wailed in distress:
'How strange that they should have made this decision!
We cannot.fathom the doings of Tiamat!'
They made ready to leave on their journey,
All the great gods who decree the fates.
They entered before Anshar, filling Ubshukinna.
They kissed one another in the Assembly.
They held converse as they sat down to the banquet.
They ate festive bread, partook of the wine,
They wetted their drinking tubes with sweet intoxicant.
As they drank the strong drink their bodies swelled.
They became very languid as their spirits rose.
For Marduk, their avenger, they fixed the decrees.
They erected for him a princely throne.
Facing his fathers, he sat down, presiding.
'Thou art the most honoured of the great gods,
Thy decree is unrivalled, thy command is Anu.[22]
Thou, Marduk, art the most honoured of the great gods.
....
We have granted thee Kingship over the universe entire.
When in the Assembly thou sittest, thy word shall be supreme.
Thy weapons shall not fail; they shall smash thy foes!
O lord, spare the life of him who trusts thee,
But pour out the life of the god who seized evil.'
Having placed in their midst a piece of cloth,
They addressed themselves to Marduk, their first-born:
'Lord, truly thy decree is first among gods.
Say but to wreck or create; it shall be.
Open thy mouth: the cloth will vanish!
Speak again, and the cloth shall be whole!'
At the word of his mouth the cloth vanished.
He spoke again, and the cloth was restored.

When the gods, his fathers, saw the fruit of his word,
Joyfully they did him homage: 'Marduk is king!'
They conferred on him sceptre, throne, and palū;
They gave him matchless weapons that ward off the foes:
Bel's[23] destiny thus fixed, the gods, his fathers,
Caused him to go the way of success and attainment.
He constructed a bow, marked it as his weapon,
Attached thereto the arrow, fixed its bow-cord.
He raised the mace, made his right hand grasp it;
Bow and quiver he hung at his side.
In front of him he set the lightning,
With a blazing flame he filled his body.
He then made a net to enfold Tiamat therein.
The four winds he stationed that nothing of her might escape,
The South Wind, the North Wind, the East Wind, the West Wind.
Close to his side he held the net, the gift of his father, Anu.
He brought forth Imhullu, 'the Evil Wind,' the Whirlwind, the Hurricane,
The Fourfold Wind, the Sevenfold Wind, the Cyclone, the Matchless Wind;
Then he sent forth the winds he had brought forth, the seven of them.
To stir up the inside of Tiamat they rose up behind him.
Then the lord raised up the flood-storm, his mighty weapon.
He mounted the storm-chariot irresistible and terrifying.
He harnessed (and) yoked to it a team-of-four,
The Killer, the Relentless, the Trampler, the Swift.
Sharp were their teeth, bearing poison.
They were versed in ravage, in destruction skilled.
. . . .
With his fearsome halo his head was turbaned,
The lord went forth and followed his course,
Towards the raging Tiamat he set his face.
In his lips he held [a . . .] of red paste;[24]
A plant to put out poison was grasped in his hand.
Then they milled about him, the gods milled about him.
The lord approached to scan the inside of Tiamat,
(And) of Kingu, her consort, the scheme to perceive.
As he looks on, his[25] course becomes upset,
His will is distracted and his doings are confused.
And when the gods, his helpers, who marched at his side,
Saw the valiant hero, blurred became their vision.

The Creation of the World

Tiamat uttered a cry, without turning her neck,
Framing savage defiance in her lips:
'Too important art thou for the lord of the gods to rise up against thee!
Is it in their place that they have gathered, (or) in thy place?'
Thereupon the lord having raised the flood-storm, his mighty weapon,
To enraged Tiamat he sent word as follows:
'Mightily art thou risen, art haughtily exalted;
Thou hast charged thine own heart to stir up conflict,
So that sons reject their own fathers,
And thou who hast borne them, dost hate [. . .]!
Thou hast aggrandized Kingu to be (thy) consort;
A rule, not rightfully his, thou hast substituted for the rule of Anu.
Against Anshar, king of the gods, thou seekest evil;
Against the gods, my fathers, thou hast confirmed thy wickedness.
Though drawn up be thy forces, girded on thy weapons,
Stand thou up, that I and thou meet in single combat!'
When Tiamat heard this,
She was like one possessed; she took leave of her senses.
In fury Tiamat cried out aloud.
To the roots her legs shook both together.
She recited a charm, keeps casting her spell,
While the gods of battle sharpen their weapons.
Then joined issue Tiamat and Marduk, wisest of gods,
They swayed in single combat, locked in battle.
The lord spread out his net to enfold her,
The Evil Wind, which followed behind, he let loose in her face.
When Tiamat opened her mouth to consume him,
He drove in the Evil Wind that she close not her lips.
As the fierce winds charged her belly,
Her body was distended and her mouth was wide open.
He released the arrow, it tore her belly,
It cut through her insides, splitting the heart.
Having thus subdued her, he extinguished her life.
He cast down her carcass to stand upon it.
After he had slain Tiamat, the leader,
Her band was shattered, her troupe broken up.

[Tiamat's helpers panic and run, but Marduk captures and fetters all of them.]

And Kingu, who had been made chief among them,
He bound and accounted him to Uggae.[26]

He took from him the Tablets of Fate, not rightfully his,
Sealed (them) with a seal[27] and fastened (them) on his breast.
When he had vanquished and subdued his adversaries,
....

And turned back to Tiamat whom he had bound.
The lord trod on the legs of Tiamat,
With his unsparing mace he crushed her skull.
When the arteries of her blood he had severed,
The North Wind bore (it) to places undisclosed.
On seeing this, his fathers were joyful and jubilant,
They brought gifts of homage, they to him.
Then the lord paused to view her dead body,
That he might divide the monster and do artful works.
He split her like a shellfish into two parts:
Half of her he set up and ceiled as sky,
Pulled down the bar and posted guards.
He bade them to allow not her waters to escape.
He crossed the heavens and surveyed (its) regions.
He squared Apsu's quarter, the abode of Nudimmud,
As the lord measured the dimensions of Apsu.
The Great Abode, its likeness, he fixed as Esharra,
The Great Abode, Esharra, which he made as the firmament.
Anu, Enlil,[28] and Ea he made occupy their places.

[Much of Tablet V is broken. Marduk puts the heavens in order,
establishing the zodiac and telling the moon how to shine.]

When Marduk hears the words of the gods,
His heart prompts (him) to fashion artful works.
Opening his mouth, he addresses Ea
To impart the plan he addresses Ea
To impart the plan he had conceived in his heart:
'Blood I will mass and cause bones to be.
I will establish a savage, "man" shall be his name.
Verily, savage-man I will create.
He shall be charged with the service of the gods
    That they might be at ease!
The ways of the gods I will artfully alter.
Though alike revered, into two (groups) they shall be divided.'
Ea answered him, speaking a word to him,
To relate to him a scheme for the relief of the gods:
'Let but one of their brothers be handed over;

He alone shall perish that mankind may be fashioned.[29]
Let the great gods be here in Assembly,
Let the guilty be handed over that they may endure.'
Marduk summoned the great gods to Assembly;
Presiding graciously, he issued instructions.
To his utterance the gods pay heed.
The king addresses a word to the Anunnaki:
'If your former statement was true,
Do (now) the truth on oath by me declare!
Who was it that contrived the uprising,
And made Tiamat rebel, and joined battle?
Let him be handed over who contrived the uprising.
His guilt I will make him bear that you may dwell in peace!'
The Igigi, the great gods, replied to him,
To Lugaldimmerankia,[30] counsellor of the gods, their lord:
'It was Kingu who contrived the uprising,
And made Tiamat rebel, and joined battle.'
They bound him, holding him before Ea.
They imposed on him his guilt and severed his blood (vessels).
Out of his blood they fashioned mankind.
He[31] imposed the service and let free the gods.

[After the creation of mankind, Marduk divides the Anunnaki and
assigns them to their proper stations, three hundred in heaven, three
hundred on the earth.]

After he had ordered all the instructions,
To the Anunnaki of heaven and earth had allotted their portions,
The Anunnaki opened their mouths
And said to Marduk, their lord:
'Now, O lord, thou who hast caused our deliverance,
What shall be our homage to thee?
Let us build a shrine to thee whose name shall be called
'Lo, a chamber for our nightly rest'; let us repose in it!
Let us build a shrine, a recess for his abode!
On the day that we arrive[32] we shall repose in it.'
When Marduk heard this,
Brightly glowed his features, like the day:
'Like that of lofty Babylon, whose building you have requested,
Let its brickwork be fashioned. You shall name it "The Sanctuary." '
The Anunnaki applied the implement;
For one whole year they moulded bricks.

When the second year arrived,
They raised high the head of Esagila[33] equaling Apsu.[34]
Having built a stage-tower as high as Apsu,
They set up in it an abode for Marduk, Enlil, (and) Ea.
In their presence he adorned (it) in grandeur.
To the base of Esharra its horns look down.
After they had achieved the building of Esagila,
The Anunnaki themselves erected their shrines.
[. . .] all of them gathered,
[. . .] they had built as his dwelling.
The gods, his fathers, at his banquet he seated:
'This is Babylon, the place that is your home!
Make merry in its precincts, occupy its broad places.'
The great gods took their seats,
They set up festive drink, sat down to a banquet.
After they had made merry within it,
In Esagila, the splendid, had performed their rites,
The norms had been fixed (and) all their portents,
All the gods apportioned the stations of heaven and earth.
The fifty great gods took their seats.
The seven gods of destiny set up the three hundred in heaven.
Enlil raised the bow, his weapon, and laid (it) before them.
The gods, his fathers, saw the net he had made.
When they beheld the bow, how skilful its shape,
His fathers praised the work he had wrought.
Raising (it), Anu spoke up in the Assembly of the gods,
As he kissed the bow:

[The remainder of the epic is a long hymn of praise to Marduk.
It culminates in a recitation of his fifty names, attributes reflecting
his power and mighty deeds.]

Notes

1 God of subterranean waters; the primeval sweet-water ocean.
2 An epithet of Tiamat; perhaps meaning 'mother.'
3 A water-deity; the primeval salt-water ocean.
4 I.e., the fresh waters of Apsu and the marine waters of Tiamat.
5 The waters of Apsu and Tiamat.
6 The first generation of gods.
7 Gods.
8 The sky-god.
9 One of the names of Ea, the earth and water-god.
10 Ea, the earth- and water-god.

11 That of Apsu and his vizier Mummu.
12 I.e., caused it to be in the waters of Apsu.
13 'The Deep.'
14 See note 13.
15 Cf. Ezekiel 1:6.
16 The weapon of the sun-god.
17 The gods who joined Tiamat in her war.
18 Here a collective name of the nether world gods.
19 Tiamat and Kingu.
20 The assembly hall of the gods.
21 A collective name of the heaven gods.
22 I.e., it has the authority of the sky-god Anu.
23 I.e., Marduk's destiny.
24 Red being the magic colour for warding off evil influence.
25 I.e., Kingu's course.
26 God of death.
27 By this action Marduk legalized his ownership of the Tablets of Fate.
28 The god of the wind, i.e., of the earth.
29 Out of his blood.
30 Meaning 'The king of the gods of heaven and earth.'
31 Ea.
32 For the New Year's Festival.
33 Name of the temple of Marduk in Babylon.
34 Meaning apparently that the height of Esagila corresponded to the depth of Apsu's waters.

Translation by E. A. Speiser, in *Ancient Near Eastern Texts* (Princeton, 1950), pp. 60-72, as reprinted in Isaac Mendelsohn (ed.), *Religions of the Ancient Near East*, Library of Religion, paperbook series (New York, 1955), pp. 19-46; notes by Mendelsohn

56. 'WHO CAN SAY WHENCE IT ALL CAME, AND HOW CREATION HAPPENED?'

('Rig Veda,' X, 129)

This creation hymn is at once a supreme expression of the poetry and philosophy of the Rig Veda and an eloquent murmur of doubt, which carries over into the Upanishads its sense of the depth, the mystery, and above all the unity of creation. In 'darkness concealed in darkness' (tamas in tamas), in those 'unillumined waters' which harbour no 'being' (sat) or 'non-being' (asat), there is generated, by cosmic heat (tapas) the primordial unitary force, That One (tad ekam). 'Desire' (kāma) now arose as the primal seed of 'mind' (manas), the firstborn of tad ekam, and the rishis, who 'see' that original moment when the gods were not, claim now to know the bond of sat in asat. 'But who knows truly,' concludes the poet, still in reverence before the mystery: perhaps That One 'whose eye controls this world'; but then perhaps he truly does not know.

Not only Upanshadic speculation, but also the evolutionary philosophy of the Sāmkhya system was deeply impressed by this hymn. It is important to consider this speculation of cosmic origins alongside other Rig Vedic creation accounts, such as X, 90 and X, 112 or I, 32.

1. Then[1] even nothingness was not, nor existence.[2]
     There was no air then, nor the heavens beyond it.
   What covered it? Where was it? In whose keeping?
     Was there then cosmic water, in depths unfathomed?
2. Then there were neither death nor immortality,
     nor was there then the torch of night and day.
   The One[3] breathed windlessly and self-sustaining.[4]
     There was that One then, and there was no other.
3. At first there was only darkness wrapped in darkness.
     All this was only unillumined water.[5]
   That One which came to be, enclosed in nothing,
     arose at last, born of the power of heat.[6]
4. In the beginning desire descended on it—
     that was the primal seed, born of the mind.
   The sages who have searched their hearts with wisdom
     know that which is, is kin[7] to that which is not.
5. And they have stretched their cord across the void,
     and know what was above, and what below.
   Seminal powers made fertile mighty forces.
     Below was strength, and over it was impulse.[8]
6. But, after all, who knows, and who can say
     whence it all came, and how creation happened?
   The gods themselves are later than creation,
     so who knows truly whence it has arisen?
7. Whence all creation had its origin,
     he, whether he fashioned it or whether he did not,
   he, who surveys it all from highest heaven,
     he knows—or maybe even he does not know.

Notes

1 In the beginning.
2 *Asat* nor *sat.*
3 *Tad ekam,* 'That One,' who 'breathes without air.'
4 *Svadhā,* energy, intrinsic power which makes self-generation possible.
5 Fluid (*salila*) and indistinguishable (*apraketa*)
6 *Tapas,* an archaic word which also defines those human austerities or techniques which, like this cosmic heat, generate power.
7 From 'bond' (*bandhu*).
8 This stanza is obscure. A. A. Macdonell suggests that the 'cord' (*rashmi*) implies the bond of the preceding stanza; thought measures out the distance between the non-existent and the existent and separates the male and female cosmogonic principles: impulse (*prayati*) above and energy (*svadhā*) below. (A *Vedic Reader for Students,* London: Oxford University, 1917, p. 210.)

Translation by A. L. Basham, *The Wonder That Was India* (London, 1954), pp. 247-8

See also *nos.* 101, 292-4, 300

57. INDIAN COSMOGONY

('The Laws of Manu,' 1, 5-16)

The Mānavadharmashāstra or Manusmriti, *known in the West as* The Laws of Manu *is the most important work regarding dharma, i.e., the principles, laws, and rules governing both the cosmos and human society. The dates assigned by scholars for the composition of the text vary from the second century* B.C. *to the second century* A.D. *The cosmogonic fragment reprinted below is known to be a late interpolation.*

5. This (universe) existed in the shape of Darkness,[1] unperceived, destitute of distinctive marks, unattainable by reasoning, unknowable, wholly immersed, as it were, in deep sleep.

6. Then the divine Self-existent[2] indiscernible, (but) making (all) this, the great elements and the rest, discernible, appeared with irresistible (creative) power, dispelling the darkness.

7. He who can be perceived by the internal organ[3] (alone), who is subtle, indiscernible, and eternal, who contains all created beings and is inconceivable, shone forth of his own (will).[4]

8. He, desiring to produce beings of many kinds from his own body, first with a thought created[5] the waters, and placed [his] seed in them.

9. That (seed) became a golden egg,[6] in brilliancy equal to the sun; in that (egg) he himself was born as Brahmán, the progenitor of the whole world.

10. The waters were called *nārās*, (for) the waters are, indeed, the offspring of Nara; as they were his[7] first residence *(ayana)*, he thence is named Nārāyana.[8]

11. From that (first) cause, which is indiscernible, eternal, and both real and unreal,[9] was produced that male (Purusha),[10] who is famed in this world (under the appellation of) Brahmán.

12. The divine one resided in that egg during a whole year,[11] then he himself by his thought[12] (alone) divided it into two halves;

13. And out of those two halves he formed heaven and earth, between them the middle sphere, the eight points of the horizon, and the eternal abode of the waters.

14. From himself (ātmanas) he also drew forth the mind,[31] which is both real and unreal, likewise from the mind egoism,[14] which possesses the function of self-consciousness (and is) lordly:

15. Moreover, the great one,[15] the soul,[16] and all products affected by the three qualities,[17] and, in their order, the five organs which perceive the objects of sensation.[18]

16. But, joining minute particles even of those six,[19] which possess measureless power, with particles of himself he created all beings.

Notes

1 *Tamas*, a darkness both physical and mental. The Sāmkhya system finds considerable significance in this stanza: *tamas*, one of the three twisted strands *(gunas)* of cosmic substance, represents inertia.

2 *Svayambhū*, an epithet of Brahmán (masculine), who is the impersonal Absolute (Bráhman neuter) personified as manifest god.

3 *Atīndriya*, literally that spirit or mind 'beyond the senses.'

4 I.e., became self-manifest.

5 Or, released.

6 As 'the shape of Darkness' (vs. 1) and the environmental 'waters' recall the Rig Vedic creation hymn X, 120, so does this golden 'egg' *(anda)* and its seed *(bīja)* recall the *hiranyagarbha* of *Rig Veda*, X, 121.

7 Brahmán's.

8 An example of popular etymology, *nara* being primal man or eternal spirit.

9 Literally, having existence *(sat)* and non-existence *(asat)* as its nature.

10 See the Purushasūkta, *Rig Veda*, X, 90.

11 Early commentators disagreed, some saying that the 'year' was a 'year of Brahmán,' others maintaining that a human year is meant, as in the similar version of this selection, *Shatapatha-brāhmana*, XI, 1, 6, 1 *ff.*

12 Meditation (*dhyāna*).

13 *Manas*, mind or intelligence, as distinct from spirit (*ātman*).

14 *Ahamkāra*, literally 'the making of "I" (*aham*)'; the principle of individuation.

15 *Mahat*, the 'great'; in Sāmkhya also called *buddhi*, consciousness.

16 *Ātman*.

17 *Gunas*.

18 *Tanmātras*, subtle elements.

19 Again, the Indian commentators are at variance in their interpretations of these last three lines. Probably 'those six' are classes of *tattvas* (elements) mentioned in the preceding two verses, in the order: *manas, ahamkāra, mahat, ātman, tattvas* affected by the *gunas, tanmatras*. It is interesting to compare the Sāmkya evolutes of *prakriti*. Here twenty-five *tattvas*, a rearrangement of 'those six' above, evolve with greater systematization: (1) *purusha*; and from *prakriti*, (2) *mahat*, (3) *ahamkāra*, (4) *manas*, (5) five sense organs and five motor organs, (6) five subtle elements (*tanmātras*) and five gross elements (*mahābhūtas*).

Translation by G. Bühler, in *Sacred Books of the East,* xxv (Oxford, 1886), pp. 2-8

58. THE CREATION OF THE WORLD ACCORDING TO THE UPANISHADS

1. There was nothing whatsoever here in the beginning. By death indeed was this covered, or by hunger, for hunger is death. He created the mind, thinking 'let me have a self' (mind). Then he moved about, worshipping. From him, thus worshipping, water was produced. . . .

2. . . . That which was the froth of the water became solidified; that became the earth. On it he [i.e., death] rested. From him thus rested and heated (from the practice of austerity) his essence of brightness came forth (as) fire.

3. He divided himself threefold (fire is one-third), the sun one-third and the air one-third. He also is life [lit., breath] divided threefold, . . . (Brihad-āranyaka Upanishad, I, 2, 1-3.)

1. The Sun is *Brahman*—this is the teaching. An explanation thereof (is this). In the beginning this (world) was non-existent. It became existent. It grew. It turned into an egg. It lay for the period of a year. It burst open. Then came out of the eggshell, two parts, one of silver, the other of gold.

That which was of silver is this earth; that which was of gold is the sky. What was the outer membrane is the mountains; that which was the inner membrane is the mist with the clouds. What were the veins were the rivers. What was the fluid within is the ocean. (*Chāndogya Upanishad,* III, 19, 1-2.)

[*But further on, the sage Uddalaka presents another view: in the beginning was Being alone.*]

1. In the beginning, my dear, this was Being alone, one only without a second. Some people say 'in the beginning this was non-being alone, one only; without a second. From that non-being, being was produced.'

2. But how, indeed, my dear, could it be thus? said he [i.e., the sage Uddalaka], how could being be produced from non-being? On the contrary, my dear, in the beginning this was being alone, one only, without a second.

3. It thought, May I be many, may I grow forth. It sent forth fire. That fire thought, May I be many, may I grow forth. It sent forth water. . . .

4. That water thought, May I be many, may I grow forth. It sent forth food. . . . (*Chāndogya Upanishad,* VI, 2, 1-4.)

S. Radhakrishnan (editor and translator), *The Principal Upanishads* (New York: Harper & Row, 1953), pp. 151-2, 399, 447-9

59. HESIOD'S THEOGONY AND COSMOGONY

('Theogony,' 116-210)

The main themes of Hesiod's 'Theogony' are (1) the coming into being of Chaos (the Void), Earth, Eros, Sky and the first generation of gods (lines 116-53); (2) the castration of Sky by his son Cronus, instigated by his mother Earth (lines 154-210); (3) Zeus' escape from being swallowed by his father Cronus (lines 453-500); (4) the victorious battle of Zeus and the Olympian gods against the Titans (lines 617-735). Only the first two episodes are printed below. It is impossible to determine Hesiod's date, but he is later than Homer, probably eighth century B.C. The similarities to and differences from the Ancient Near East cosmogonies are discussed by Norman O. Brown in the introduction to his translation, 'Hesiod's Theogony,' pp. 36 ff.

The Creation of the World

First of all, the Void (*Chaos*) came into being, next broad-bosomed Earth, the solid and eternal home of all, and Eros [Desire], the most beautiful of the immortal gods, who in every man and every god softens the sinews and overpowers the prudent purpose of the mind. Out of Void came Darkness and black Night, and out of Night came Light and Day, her children conceived after union in love with Darkness. Earth first produced starry Sky, equal in size with herself, to cover her on all sides. Next she produced the tall mountains, the pleasant haunts of the gods, and also gave birth to the barren waters, sea with its raging surges—all this without the passion of love. Thereafter she lay with Sky and gave birth to Ocean with its deep current. Coeus and Crius and Hyperion and Iapetus; Thea and Rhea and Themia [Law] and Mnemosyne [Memory]; also golden-crowned Phoebe and lovely Tethys. After these came cunning Cronus, the youngest and boldest of her children; and he grew to hate the father who had begotten him.

Earth also gave birth to the violent Cyclopes—Thunderer, Lightner, and bold Flash—who made and gave to Zeus the thunder and the lightning bolt. They were like the gods in all respects except that a single eye stood in the middle of their foreheads, and their strength and power and skill were in their hands.

There were also born to Earth and Sky three more children, big, strong, and horrible, Cottus and Briareus and Gyes. This unruly brood had a hundred monstrous hands sprouting from their shoulders, and fifty heads on top of their shoulders growing from their sturdy bodies. They had monstrous strength to match their huge size.

Of all the children born of Earth and Sky these were the boldest, and their father hated them from the beginning. As each of them was about to be born, Sky would not let them reach the light of day; instead he hid them all away in the bowels of Mother Earth. Sky took pleasure in doing this evil thing. In spite of her enormous size, Earth felt the strain within her and groaned. Finally she thought of an evil and cunning stratagem. She instantly produced a new metal, grey steel, and made a huge sickle. Then she laid the matter before her children; the anguish in her heart made her speak boldly; 'My children, you have a savage father; if you will listen to me, we may be able to take vengeance for this evil outrage: he was the one who started using violence.'

This was what she said: but all the children were gripped by fear, and not one of them spoke a word. Then great Cronus, the cunning

115

trickster, took courage and answered his good mother with these words: 'Mother, I am willing to undertake and carry through your plan. I have no respect for our infamous father, since he was the one who started using violence.'

This was what he said, and enormous Earth was very pleased. She hid him in ambush and put in his hands the sickle with jagged teeth, and instructed him fully in her plot. Huge Sky came drawing night behind him and desiring to make love; he lay on top of Earth stretched all over her. Then from his ambush his son reached out with his left hand and with his right took the huge sickle with its long jagged teeth and quickly sheared the organs from his own father and threw them away. The drops of blood that spurted from them were all taken in by Mother Earth, and in the course of the revolving years she gave birth to the powerful Erinyes [Spirits of Vengeance] and the huge Giants with shining armour and long spears. As for the organs themselves, for a long time they drifted round the sea just as they were when Cronus cut them off with the steel edge and threw them from the land into the waves of the ocean; then white foam issued from the divine flesh, and in the foam a girl began to grow. First she came near to holy Cythera, then reached Cyprus, the land surrounded by sea. There she stepped out, a goddess, tender and beautiful, and round her slender feet the green grass shot up. She is called Aphrodite by gods and men because she grew in the froth, and also Cytherea, because she came near to Cythera, and the Cyprian, because she was born in watery Cyprus. Eros [Desire] and beautiful Passion were her attendants both at her birth and at her first going to join the family of the gods. The rights and privileges assigned to her from the beginning and recognized by men and gods are these; to preside over the whispers and smiles and tricks which girls employ, and the sweet delight and tenderness of love.

Great Father Sky called his children the Titans, because of his feud with them: he said that they blindly had tightened the noose and had done a savage thing for which they would have to pay in time to come.

Translation by Norman O. Brown, in his *Hesiod's Theogony* (New York: Liberal Arts Press, 1953), pp. 56-9

The Creation of the World

60. ZOROASTRIAN DUALIST COSMOGONY: OHRMAZD AND AHRIMAN

('Greater Bundahishn,' I, 18-26)

The story of the two primal Spirits and the creation of the world is recounted in greatest detail in the first chapter of a ninth-century Pahlavi book known as the 'Bundahishn' or '(Book of) the Primal Creation.' The limitation of Time is Ohrmazd's first creative act, for he saw that if Ahriman were to be destroyed, he would have to be lured out of eternity, actualized in finite time, and forced into the open.

18. Ohrmazd, before the act of creation, was not Lord; after the act of creation he became Lord, eager for increase, wise, free from adversity, manifest, ever ordering aright, bounteous, all-perceiving. 19. [First he created the essence of the gods, fair (orderly) movement, that genius by which he made his own body better] for he had conceived of the act of creation; from this act of creation was his lordship.

20. And by his clear vision Ohrmazd saw that the Destructive Spirit would never cease from aggression and that his aggression could only be made fruitless by the act of creation, and that creation could not move on except through Time and that when Time was fashioned, the creation of Ahriman too would begin to move. 21. And that he might reduce the Aggressor to a state of powerlessness, having no alternative he fashioned forth Time. And the reason was this, that the Destructive Spirit could not be made powerless unless he were brought to battle. . . .

22. Then from Infinite Time he fashioned and made Time of the long Dominion: some call it finite Time. From Time of the long Dominion he brought forth permanence that the works of Ohrmazd might not pass away. From permanence discomfort was made manifest that comfort might not touch the demons. From discomfort the course of fate, the idea of changelessness, was made manifest, that those things which Ohrmazd created at the original creation might not change. From the idea of changelessness a perfect will (to create) material creation was made manifest, the concord of the righteous creation.

23. In his unrighteous creation Ahriman was without knowledge, without method. And the reason and interpretation thereof is this,

117

that when Ahriman joined battle with Ohrmazd the majestic wisdom, renown, perfection, and permanence of Ohrmazd and the powerlessness, self-will, imperfection and slowness in knowledge of the Destructive Spirit were made manifest when creation was created.

24. For Time of the long Dominion was the first creature that he fashioned forth; for it was infinite before the contamination of the totality of Ohrmazd. From the infinite it was fashioned finite; for from the original creation when creation was created until the consummation when the Destructive Spirit is made powerless there is a term of twelve thousand years which is finite. Then it mingles with and returns to the Infinite so that the creation of Ohrmazd shall for ever be with Ohrmazd in purity. 25. As it is said in the Religion, 'Time is mightier than both creations—the creation of Ohrmazd and that of the Destructive Spirit. Time understands all action and order (the law). Time understands more than those who understand. Time is better informed than the well-informed; for through Time must the decision be made. By Time are houses overturned—doom is through Time—and things graven shattered. From it no single mortal man escapes, not though he fly above, not though he dig a pit below and settle therein, not though he hide beneath a well of cold waters.'

26. From his own essence which is material light Ohrmazd fashioned forth the form of his creatures—a form of fire—bright, white, round and manifest afar. From the material (form) of that Spirit which dispels aggression in the two worlds—be it Power or be it Time—he fashioned forth the form of Vāy, the Good, for Vāy was needed: some call it Vāy of the long Dominion. With the aid of Vāy of the long Dominion he fashioned forth creation; for when he created creation, Vāy was the instrument he needed for the deed.

Translation and introductory comment by R. C. Zaehner, in his *Zurvan: A Zoroastrian Dilemma* (Oxford, 1955), pp. 314-16

See also nos. 37-9, 290, 303

B. A MYTH OF BEGINNING AND END

61. THE SCANDINAVIAN STORY OF CREATION AND A PROPHECY OF THE END OF THE WORLD

('Völuspá')

In the Elder, or Poetic, Edda the historian of religions finds no greater fascination than that of the Völuspá—the 'Sibyl's Prophecy.' In a few succinct verses this highly original poem of the gods sets forth a world view that sweeps powerfully from a vision of primordial chaos and creation through the turbulent lives of the gods to their ultimate doom in the ragnarök.

The poem is profoundly Scandinavian. A dark foreboding pursues each line as the poet unfolds the story of the world, told by a völva (a sibyl or seeress) whom the sovereign god Odin, maker of magic and lord of the dead, has called forth from the grave. The völva, abrupt and dramatic in her sombre vision, 'sees' first the abyss, Ginnungagap, in that age when sea and 'earth had not been, nor heaven above.' Chaos gives way to cosmos through the efforts of the gods, and soon giants, dwarfs and humans dwell on earth. The golden age of the young gods is terminated, however, when the first war—between the Æsir and the Vanir—takes its fateful course.

Like the Norns (the three goddesses who span past, present, and future), the sibyl 'sees' as well that which is to come, and to Odin she now describes the ragnorök, the 'fate of the gods.' The tribal battle has exploded into a great cosmic struggle between good and evil, light and darkness, harmony and chaos, life and death. Earth cannot bear this war and the völva's apocalyptic visions now portend its destruction by fire and flood. The world-tree Yggdrasill is shaken to the roots, the innocent god Baldr and then Odin himself are slain, 'the sun turns black, earth sinks in the sea,' and 'fire leaps high about heaven itself.'

Before the völva sinks again into earth, however, she concludes her vision with a scene of rebirth: 'Now do I see the earth anew/Rise all green from the waves again.' Baldr returns, the earth is fruitful, and a new golden hall of the gods appears.

The possibility of some influence from Christian symbolism, particularly in the final verses, has suggested a date of composition in the late tenth or early eleventh century, when Christianity began to penetrate the final northern frontiers. However, the Völuspá—terse, mystical, often obscure—has a unique perspective, and it survives for us as a last magnificent expression from an expiring heroic age.

1. Hearing I ask / from the holy races,
   From Heimdall's sons, / both high and low;
   Thou wilt, Valfather, / that well I relate
   Old tales I remember / of men long ago.

2. I remember yet / the giants of yore,
   Who gave me bread / in the days gone by;
   Nine worlds I knew, / the nine in the tree
   With mighty roots / beneath the mould.

3. Of old was the age / when Ymir lived;
   Sea nor cool waves / nor sand there were;
   Earth had not been, / nor heaven above,
   But a yawning gap, / and grass nowhere.

4. Then Bur's sons lifted / the level land,
   Midgard the mighty / there they made;
   The sun from the south / warmed the stones of earth,
   And green was the ground / with growing leeks.

5. The sun, the sister / of the moon, from the south
   Her right hand cast / over heaven's rim;
   No knowledge she had / where her home should be,
   The moon knew not / what might was his,
   The stars knew not / where their stations were.

6. Then sought the gods / their assembly-seats
   The holy ones, / and council held;
   Names then gave they / to noon and twilight,
   Morning they named / and the waning moon,
   Night and evening, / the years to number.

7. At Idavöll met / the mighty gods,
   Shrines and temples / they timbered high;
   Forges they set, / and they smithied ore,
   Tongs they wrought, / and tools they fashioned.

8. In their dwellings at peace   they played at tables,
   Of gold no lack   did the gods then know,—
   Till thither came up   giant-maids three,
   Huge of might,   out of Jötunheim.

9. Then sought the gods   their assembly-seats
   The holy ones,   and council held,
   To find who should raise   the race of dwarfs
   Out of Brimir's blood   and the legs of Blain. . . .

17. Then from the throng   did three come forth
    From the home of the gods,   the mighty and gracious;
    Two without fate   on the land they found,
    Ask and Embla,   empty of might.

18. Soul they had not,   sense they had not,
    Heat nor motion,   nor goodly hue;
    Soul gave Odin,   sense gave Hönir,
    Heat gave Lodur   and goodly hue.

19. An ash I know,   Yggdrasill its name,
    With water white   is the great tree wet;
    Thence come the dews   that fall in the dales,
    Green by Urd's well   does it ever grow.

20. Thence come the maidens   mighty in wisdom,
    Three from the dwelling   down 'neath the tree;
    Urd is one named,   Verdandi the next,—
    On the wood they scored,—   And Skuld the third.
    Laws they made there,   and life allotted
    To the sons of men,   and set their fates.

21. The war I remember,   the first in the world,
    When the gods with spears   had smitten Gullveig.
    And in the hall   of Har had burned her,—
    Three times burned,   and three times born,
    Oft and again,   yet ever she lives.

22. Heid they named her   who sought their home
    The wide-seeing witch   in magic wise;
    Minds she bewitched   that were moved by her magic,
    To evil women   a joy she was.

23. On the host his spear   did Odin hurl
    Then in the world   did war first come;

The wall that girdled   the gods was broken,
And the field by the warlike   Vanir was trodden.

24. Then sought the gods   their assembly-seats
     The holy ones,   and council held,
     Whether the gods   should tribute give,
     Or to all alike   should worship belong.

25. Then sought the gods   their assembly-seats,
     The holy ones,   and council held,
     To find who with venom   the air had filled,
     Or had given Od's bride   to the giants' brood.

26. In swelling rage   then rose up Thor,—
     Seldom he sits   when he such things hears,—
     And the oaths were broken,   the words and bonds,
     The mighty pledges   between them made.

27. I know of the horn   of Heimdall, hidden
     Under the high-reaching   holy tree;
     On it there pours   from Valfather's pledge
     A mighty stream: would you know yet more?

28. Alone I sat   when the Old One sought me,
     The terror of gods,   and gazed in mine eyes;
     'What hast thou to ask?   why comest thou hither?
     Odin, I know   where thine eye is hidden.'

29. I know where Odin's   eye is hidden,
     Deep in the wide-famed   well of Mimir;
     Mead from the pledge   of Odin each morn
     Does Mimir drink: would you know yet more?

30. Necklaces had I   and rings from Heerfather,
     Wise was my speech   and my magic wisdom;
     ....
     Widely I saw   over all the worlds.

31. On all sides saw I   Valkyries assemble
     Ready to ride   to the ranks of the gods;
     Skuld bore the shield,   and Skögul rode next,
     Gud, Hild, Gondul   and Geirskögul.
     Of Herjan's maidens   the list have ye heard,
     Valkyries ready   to ride o'er the earth.

32. I saw for Baldr,   the bleeding god,
    The sons of Odin,   his destiny set:
    Famous and fair   in the lofty fields,
    Full grown in strength the mistletoe stood.

33. From the branch which
    seemed   so slender and fair
    Came a harmful shaft   that Höd should hurl;
    But the brother of Baldr was born ere long.
    And one night old   fought Odin's son.

34. His hands he washed not, his hair he combed not,
    Till he bore to the bale-blaze Baldr's foe
    But in Fensalir   did Frigg weep sore
    For Valhall's need: would you know yet more?

35. One did I see   in the wet woods bound
    A lover of ill,   and to Loki like;
    By his side does Sigyn   sit, nor is glad
    To see her mate: would you know yet more?

36. From the east there pours through poisoned vales
    With swords and daggers the river Slid.
    ....
    ....

37. Northward a hall   in Nidavellir
    Of gold there rose   for Sindri's race;
    And in Okolnir   another stood.
    Where the giant Brimir   his beer-hall had.

38. A hall I saw,   far from the sun.
    On Naströnd it stands   and the doors face north;
    Venom drops   through the smoke-vent down,
    For around the walls   do serpents wind.

39. I saw there wading   through rivers wild
    Treacherous men   and murderers too,
    And workers of ill   with the wives of men;
    There Nidhögg sucked   the blood of the slain,
    And the wolf tore men; would you know yet more?

40. The giantess old   in Ironwood sat,
    In the east, and bore   the brood of Fenrir;
    Among these one   in monster's guise
    Was soon to steal   the sun from the sky.

123

41. There feeds he full   on the flesh of the dead,
And the home of the gods   he reddens with gore;
Dark grows the sun,   and in summer soon
Come mighty storms: would you know yet more?

42. On a hill there sat,   and smote on his harp
Eggther the joyous   the giants' warder;
Above him the cock   in the bird-wood crowed,
Fair and red   did Fjalar stand.

43. Then to the gods   crowed Gollinkambi,
He wakes the heroes   in Odin's hall;
And beneath the earth   does another crow,
The rust-red bird   at the bars of Hel.

44. Now Garm howls loud   before Gnipahellir,
The fetters will burst,   and the wolf run free;
Much do I know,   and more can see
Of the fate of the gods,   the mighty in fight.

45. Brothers shall fight   and fell each other,
And sisters' sons   shall kinship stain;
Hard is it on earth,   with mighty whoredom;
Axe-time, sword-time,   shields are sundered,
Wind-time, wolf-time,   ere the world falls;
Nor ever shall men   each other spare.

46. Fast move the sons   of Mim, and fate
Is heard in the note   of the Gjallarhorn;
Loud blows Heimdall,   the horn is aloft,
In fear quake all   who on Hel-roads are.

47. Yggdrasill shakes,   and shiver on high
The ancient limbs   and the giant is loose;
To the head of Mim   does Odin give heed,
But the kinsman of Surt   shall slay him soon.

48. How fare the gods?   how fare the elves?
All Jötunheim groans,   the gods are at council;
Loud roar the dwarfs   by the doors of stone,
The masters of the rocks: would you know yet more?

49. Now Garm howls loud   before Gnipahellir,
The fetters will burst,   and the wolf run free;
Much do I know,   and more can see
Of the fate of the gods,   the mighty in fight.

50. From the east comes Hrym   with shield held high;
    In giant-wrath   does the serpent writhe;
    O'er the waves he twists,   and the tawny eagle
    Gnaws corpses screaming;   Naglfar is loose.

51. O'er the sea from the north there sails a ship
    With the people of Hel,   at the helm stands Loki;
    After the wolf   do wild men follow,
    And with them the brother   of Byleist goes.

52. Surt fares from the south   with the scourge of branches,
    The sun of the battle-gods   shone from his sword;
    The crags are sundered   the giant-women sink,
    The dead throng Hel-way,   and heaven is cloven.

53. Now comes to Illin   yet another hurt,
    When Odin fares   to fight with the wolf,
    And Beli's fair slayer   seeks out Surt,
    For there must fall   the joy of Frigg.

54. Then comes Sigfather's   mighty son,
    Vidar, to fight   with the foaming wolf;
    In the giant's son   does he thrust his sword
    Full to the heart: his father is avenged.

55. Hither there comes   the son of Heöthyn,
    The bright snake gapes   to heaven above;
    ....
    Against the serpent   goes Odin's son.

56. In anger smites   the warder of the earth—
    Forth from their homes   must all men flee,—
    Nine paces fares   the son of Fjörgyn.
    And, slain by the serpent,   fearless he sinks.

57. The sun turns black,   earth sinks in the sea,
    The hot stars down   from heaven are whirled;
    Fierce grows the steam   and the life-feeding flame,
    Till fire leaps high   about heaven itself.

58. Now Garm howls loud   before Gnipahellir,
    The fetters will burst,   and the wolf run free;
    Much do I know,   and more can see
    Of the fate of the gods,   the mighty in fight.

59. Now do I see   the earth anew
  Rise all green   from the waves again;
  The cataracts fall, and the eagle flies,
  And fish he catches beneath the cliffs.

60. The gods in Idavoll meet together,
  Of the terrible girdler of earth they talk.
  And the mighty past they call to mind,
  And the ancient runes of the Ruler of Gods.

61. In wondrous beauty once again
  Shall the golden tables stand mid the grass,
  Which the gods had owned in the days of old,
  . . . .

62. Then fields unsowed bear ripened fruit,
  All ills grow better, and Baldr comes back;
  Baldr and Höd dwell in Hropt's battle-hall,
  And the mighty gods: would you know yet more?

63. Then Hönir wins   the prophetic wand,
  . . . .
  And the sons of the brothers of Tveggi abide
  In Vindheim now: would you know yet more?

64. More fair than the sun, a hall I see,
  Roofed with gold, on Gimle it stands;
  There shall the righteous rulers dwell,
  And happiness ever there shall they have.

65. There comes on high. all power to hold,
  A mighty lord,   all lands he rules.
  . . . .
  . . . .

66. From below the dragon dark comes forth,
  Nidhögg flying   from Nidafjöll;
  The bodies of men on his wings he bears
  The serpent bright: but now I must sink.

Notes (numbers refer to stanzas)

1 *Heimdall:* the watchman of the gods, son of nine giantesses, and ancestor of mankind. *Valfather:* Odin, 'Father of the Slain,' the sovereign god who receives the fallen warriors in his great palace, Valhall (*Valhöll,* 'Hall of the Slain').

A Myth of Beginning and End

2 The *völva* recalls here the cosmic tree Yggdrasill (the 'steed of Ygg [Odin]') which comprises the 'nine worlds.' We are reminded (as in stanzas 28-9) of how Odin gains occult wisdom (*seid*): he wins the secrets of the runes, nine magic songs, and the immortal drink (*mjöd*, 'mead') of poetry by hanging for nine nights on the tree and sacrificing himself to himself. The 'Rúnatals Tháttr' of the *Hávamál* (stanza 138) describes the scene:

> I know that I hung
> on the windswept tree
> for nine full nights,
> wounded with a spear
> and given to Odinn
> myself to myself; . . .

> (Trans. E. O. G. Turville-Petre, *Myth and Religion of the North* [London: Weidenfeld & Nicolson, 1964], p. 42.)

3 *Ymir:* the giant from whose body the gods create a world. His function in this account of creation is unclear.

4 *Bur:* father of Odin and of Odin's brothers, Vili and Ve. (Bur's father, Buri, was created by the primeval cow, Audumla, according to Snorri's *Edda*.) *Midgard:* the world of men, the 'middle region' lifted from the waters by the gods.

7 *Idavöll:* the stronghold of the gods; see stanza 60, after *ragnarök*.

8 *Jötunheim:* the world of the giants.

9 *Brimir* and *Blain:* two giants, or possibly, names of the giant Ymir. Stanzas 10-16, an interpolated list of dwarf names, are here omitted.

17 The 'three' here are not the giant-maids of stanza 8, but the gods Odin, Hönir, and Lodur, who proceed to create primeval man and woman, Ask and Embla ('Ash' and 'Elm').

18 To these 'trees,' 'empty of might,' Odin gives *önd* (breath, life, spirit), Hönir gives sense, and Lodur gives heat.

19 Yggdrasill, the tree of fate, stretches from the lower world to heaven. At the centre of the world, it supports the universe, and beneath its roots lies Urdar-brunnr, the well of fate.

20 From the well come the three Norns, goddesses of fate: Urd, the Past; Verdandi, the Present; Skuld, the Future. The destinies of men are carved as magic signs (runes) on wood.

21 Here commences the war between the Æsir ('gods,' singular *ass*) and the special tribe of gods known as the Vanir. Apparently an assault on the principal goddess of the Vanir, Freyja (here called Gullveig and Heid), has precipitated strife between the gods. Gullveig has been speared and burned in the palace of Har (Odin), but survives as Heid by virtue of her dark magic (*seid*).

23 Odin declares war for the Æsir by ritually hurling his magic spear. The Vanir, equipped with magic of their own, breach the wall of Asgard, the Æsir's fortress.

24 A council of all the gods now determines the tribute which the Æsir should pay for the offence against Gullveig (Freyja).

25 *Od:* the husband of Freyja.

26 *Thor:* son of Odin and Jörd, the warrior god who wields his hammer Mjöllnir against the giants and demons. The cause of Thor's outburst may have been too well known to the hearers of the *Völuspá* to bear retelling. Snorri's *Edda*

recounts how a giant, employed by the Æsir to rebuild the walls of Asgard, demands as payment the sun, the moon, and the goddess Freyja as well. After trickery on the part of the Æsir, the giant threatens and is slain by Thor, and new occasion for enmity is found.

27 Heimdall's Gjallarhorn ('Ringing Horn'), the trumpet which he uses (stanza 46) to summon the gods to battle, lies under the cosmic tree Yggdrasill. There also is hidden one of Odin's eyes, pledged to Mimir, wisest of the Æsir, in exchange for wisdom.

28 *The Old One:* Odin.

29 The *völva* knows that Odin, whose most precious sense is sight, has sacrificed an eye to the well of Mimir, and that from the eye Mimir drinks the mead of immortality. 'Would you know yet more?' comes as a taunt to Odin, who has learned the past and now awaits the hearing of his fate.

30 *Heerfather:* Odin, 'Father of the Host.'

31 *Valkyries:* 'Choosers of the Slain,' who bear the fallen warriors to Odin at Valhall. The list of warrior-maidens may be an interpolation. *Herjan:* Odin, 'Leader of the Hosts.'

32 The seeress predicts the destiny of Baldr. Like the story of Freyja and the giant builder above, the episode of Baldr's death was well known to hearers of the *Völuspá* and required only a brief résumé. From all created things, with the sole exception of the young mistletoe, Frigg had secured an oath that none would hurt Baldr, her son. Loki, the trickster among the gods, brought mistletoe to a new sport of the Æsir—throwing harmless missiles at the seemingly indestructible Baldr—and by guiding the hand of Höd, the blind brother of Baldr, he contrived the death of the young god. Odin, in grief, begets Vali ('the brother of Baldr' in stanza 33) to avenge Baldr by slaying Höd.

34 *Fensalir:* the home of Frigg, who now weeps over these days of bloodshed.

35 The *völva* sees that Loki will not escape punishment for his part in the killing of Baldr. Sigyn sits by the side of her bound mate.

36 *Slid:* a river in the world of the giants.

37 *Nidavellir:* 'Dark Fields,' the home of the dwarfs. *Sindri:* the great worker in gold among the dwarfs. *Okolnir:* 'Never Cold,' possibly a volcano. *Brimir:* see stanza 9.

38 *Naströnd:* 'Corpse-shore,' the land of the dead, ruled by the goddess Hel.

39 Here in Naströnd the *völva* sees oath-breakers and murderers undergoing dreadful punishment: Nidhögg, the devouring serpent who lives under Yggdrasill, and a wolf, probably Fenrir, a son of Loki, are their tormenters.

40 Fenrir and the nameless giantess have the wolves Skoll and Hati as their offspring; Skoll steals the sun, Hati the moon.

42 *Eggther:* apparently the watchman of the giants, as is Heimdall for the gods. The cock Fjalar in the gallows tree awakes the giants for the great battle.

43 *Gollinkambi:* 'Gold-comb,' the cock who wakes the gods in Valhall. In the world of death a 'rust-red bird' is yet a third herald of *ragnarök*.

44 The *völva* sees that Fenrir (Garm) will break loose from his den, Gnipahellir, and run free. The stanza occurs again as a refrain.

46 *Mim:* Mimir.

47 *The giant:* Fenrir. This stanza recalls the episode where two of the Æsir, Mimir and Hönir, were sent to the Vanir as hostages in a treaty of peace. The Vanir decapitated Mimir and returned the head to Odin, who thereupon preserved it and consulted it for wisdom. *Surt:* the fire-giant who rules Muspell, a world in the south; his 'kinsman' is Fenrir.

50 *Hrym:* a leader of the giants who comes as the helmsman of the giants' ship, Naglfar, made from dead men's nails. The serpent Midgardsorm, another of Loki's offspring, churns the sea.

51 Having broken from their respective fetters (stanzas 35 and 44), Loki (the brother of Byleist) and Fenrir now are en route to battle.

52 *The scourge of branches:* fire.

53 *Hlin:* Frigg, Odin's wife. *Beli's slayer:* the god Freyr, one of the Vanir and brother to Freyja, who killed the giant Beli with his fist. Odin, the 'joy of Frigg,' is destined to fall before the wolf Fenrir.

54 *Sigfather:* Odin, 'Father of Victory.' Vidar, famed for his great shield and Thor-like strength, survives destruction and avenges his father by piercing Fenrir, 'the giant's son.'

55 *Hlödyn:* Jörd ('Earth'), the mother of Thor; Thor's father was Odin. Midgardsorm is the serpent.

56 Thor is 'warder of earth' and 'son of Fjörgyn (Jörd)'; momentarily victorious over the serpent, he himself falls slain 'nine paces' away.

60 *The girdler of earth:* Midgardsorm, the serpent in the chaos waters which encircle the world. Odin is 'Ruler of Gods' and master of the runes.

61 See stanza 8, where the gods play a game resembling chess or checkers.

62 Baldr and Höd, the brother who innocently slew him, now return in the new harmonious world. *Hropt:* Odin, whose 'battle-hall' is Valhall.

63 *Hönir:* see stanza 18. In this new age he has the gift of fortelling the future. *Tveggi:* Odin, 'The Twofold,' whose brothers are Vili and Ve. *Vindheim:* heaven, 'the home of the wind.'

64 *Gimle:* a hall roofed with gold where the worthy will dwell in the new age.

65 The stanza is obscure and the new ruler is unnamed.

66 *Nidhögg:* the dragon of stanza 39. *Nidarfjöll:* the 'Dark Crags.'

Translation by Henry Adams Bellows, *The Poetic Edda* (New York: American-Scandinavian Foundation, 1923), pp. 3-6, 8-26; notes by David Knipe; translation by Turville-Petre in note 2 added by M. Eliade

C. THE CREATION OF MAN

62. THE CREATION OF WOMAN FROM THE EARTH-MOTHER (MAORI)

To produce man it was therefore necessary for the god Tane, the Fertilizer, to fashion in human form a figure of earth upon the Earth Mother's body, and to vivify it. This event transpired in the following way. (The account, according to Best, is 'rendered as given by an old native'):

Tane proceeded to the *puke* (Mons *veneris*) of Papa [the Earth] and there fashioned in human form a figure in the earth. His next task was to endow that figure with life, with human life, life as known to human beings, and it is worthy of note that, in the account of this act, he is spoken of as Tane te waiora. It was the sun light fertilizing the Earth Mother. Implanted in the lifeless image were the *wairua* (spirit) and *manawa ora* (breath of life), obtained from Io, the Supreme Being. The breath of Tane was directed upon the image, and the warmth affected it. The figure absorbed life, a faint life sigh was heard, the life spirit manifested itself, and Hine-ahu-one, the Earth Formed Maid, sneezed, opened her eyes, and rose—a woman.

Such was the Origin of Woman, formed from the substance of the Earth Mother, but animated by the divine Spirit that emanated from the Supreme Being, Io the great, Io of the Hidden Face, Io the Parent, and Io the Parentless.

E. S. Craighill Handy, *Polynesian Religion*, Bernice P. Bishop Museum Bulletin 34 (Honolulu, 1927), p. 39; quoting Elsdon Best, 'Maori Personifications,' *Journal of the Polynesian Society*, XXXII (1923), pp. 110-11

63. ZUÑI GENESIS: THE CREATION AND EMERGENCE OF MAN

A myth from the Zuñi Indians of New Mexico

Before the beginning of the new-making, Awonawilona (the Maker and Container of All, the All-father Father), solely had being. There was nothing else whatsoever throughout the great space of the ages save everywhere black darkness in it, and everywhere void desolation.

In the beginning of the new-made, Awonawilona conceived within himself and thought outward in space, whereby mists of increase, steams potent of growth, were evolved and uplifted. Thus, by means of his innate knowledge, the All-container made himself in person and form of the Sun whom we hold to be our father and who thus came to exist and appear. With his appearance came the brightening of the spaces with light, and with the brightening of the spaces the great mist-clouds were thickened together and fell, whereby was evolved water in water; yea, and the world-holding sea.

With his substance of flesh outdrawn from the surface of his person, the Sun-father formed the seed-stuff of twain worlds, impregnating therewith the great waters, and lo! in the heat of his light these waters of the sea grew green and scums rose upon them, waxing wide and weighty until, behold! they became Awitelin Tsita, the 'Four-fold Containing Mother-earth,' and Apoyan Tä'chu, the 'All-covering Father-sky.'

The Genesis of Men and the Creatures:

From the lying together of these twain upon the great world-waters, so vitalizing, terrestrial life was conceived; whence began all beings of earth, men and the creatures, in the Four-fold womb of the World.

Thereupon the Earth-mother repulsed the Sky-father, growing big and sinking deep into the embrace of the waters below, thus separating from the Sky-father in the embrace of the waters above. As a woman forebodes evil for her first-born ere born, even so did the Earth-mother forebode, long withholding from birth her myriad progeny and meantime seeking counsel with the Sky-father. 'How,' said they to one another, 'shall our children, when brought forth, know one place from another, even by the white light of the Sun-father?'

Now like all the surpassing beings the Earth-mother and the Sky-father were 'hlimna (changeable), even as smoke in the wind; transmutable at thought, manifesting themselves in any form at will, like as dancers may by mask-making.

Thus, as a man and woman, spake they, one to the other. 'Behold!' said the Earth-mother as a great terraced bowl appeared at hand and within it water, 'this is as upon me the homes of my tiny children shall be. On the rim of each world-country they wander in, terraced mountains shall stand, making in one region many, whereby country shall be known from country, and within each, place from place. Behold, again!' said she as she spat on the water and rapidly smote and stirred it with her fingers. Foam formed, gathering about the terraced rim, mounting higher and higher. 'Yea,' said she, 'and from my bosom they shall draw nourishment, for in such as this shall they find the substance of life whence we were ourselves sustained, for see!' Then with her warm breath she blew across the terraces; white flecks of the foam broke away, and, floating over above the water, were shattered by the cold breath of the Sky-father attending, and forthwith shed downward abundantly fine mist and spray! 'Even so, shall white clouds float up from the great waters at the borders of the world, and clustering about the mountain terraces of the horizons be borne aloft and abroad by the breaths of the surpassing of soul-beings, and of the children, and shall hardened and broken be by the cold, shedding downward, in rain spray, the water of life, even into the hollow places of my lap! For therein chiefly shall nestle our children mankind and creature-kind, for warmth in thy coldness.'

Lo! even the trees on high mountains near the clouds and the Sky-father crouch low towards the Earth-mother for warmth and protection! Warm is the Earth-mother, cold the Sky-father, even as woman is the warm, man the cold being!

'Even so!' said the Sky-father; 'Yet not alone shalt thou helpful be unto our children, for behold!' and he spread his hand abroad with the palm downward and into all the wrinkles and crevices thereof he set the semblance of shining yellow corn grains; in the dark of the early world-dawn they gleamed like sparks of fire, and moved as his hand was moved over the bowl, shining up from and also moving in the depths of the water therein. 'See!' said he, pointing to the seven grains clasped by his thumb and four fingers, 'by such shall our children be guided; for behold, when the Sun-father is not nigh, and thy terraces are as the dark itself (being all hidden therein), then shall our children be guided by lights—like to these lights of all the six regions turning round the midmost one—as in and around the midmost place, where these our children shall abide, lie all the other regions of space! Yea! and even as these grains gleam up from the water, so shall seed-grains like to them, yet numberless, spring up from thy bosom when touched by my waters, to nourish our children'. Thus and in other ways many devised they for their offspring.

The Creation of Man

Anon in the nethermost of the four cave-wombs of the world, the seed of men and the creatures took form and increased; even as within eggs in warm places worms speedily appear, which growing, presently burst their shells and become as may happen, birds, tadpoles or serpents, so did men and all creatures grow manifoldly and multiply in many kinds. [But these are still imperfect beings: heaped and crowded together in the darkness, they crawl over one another like reptiles, grumbling, lamenting, spitting, and using indecent and insulting language. A few among them try to escape, however. One above all, distinguished from all the others as the most intelligent is the all-sacred master, Poshaiyankya, who somehow participates in the divine condition. He emerges all alone into the light after having traversed all the four telluric cave-wombs one after another. He arrives on the surface of the Earth, which has the appearance of a vast island, wet and unstable; and he makes his way towards the Sun-father to implore him to deliver mankind and the creatures there below. The Sun then repeats the process of the creation, but this time it is creation of another order. The Sun wishes to produce intelligent, free and powerful beings. He again impregnates the foam of the Earth-mother, and from this foam twins are born. The Sun endows them with every kind of magical power and orders them to be the ancestors and lords of men.] Well instructed of the Sun-father, they lifted the Sky-father with their great cloud-bow into the vault of the high zenith, that the earth might become warm and thus fitter for their children, men and the creatures. Then along the trail of the sun-seeking Poshaiyank'ya they sped backward swiftly on their floating fog-shield, westward to the Mountain of Generation. With the magic knives of the thunderbolt they spread open the uncleft depths of the mountain, and still on their cloud-shield—even as a spider in her web descendeth—so descend they, unerringly, into the dark of the under-world. There they abode with men and the creatures, attending them, coming to know them, and becoming known of them as masters and fathers, thus seeking the ways for leading them forth.

The Birth and Delivery of Men and the Creatures:

Now there were growing things in the depths, like grasses and crawling vines. So now the Beloved Twain breathed on the stems of these grasses (growing tall, as grass is wont to do toward the light, under the opening they had cleft and whereby they had descended), causing them to increase vastly and rapidly by grasping and walking round

and round them, twisting them upward until lo! they reach forth even
into the light. And where successively they grasped the stems ridges
were formed and thumb-marks whence sprang branching leaf-stems.
Therewith the two formed a great ladder whereon men and the
creatures might ascend to the second cave-floor, and thus not be
violently ejected in after-time by the throes of the Earth-mother, and
thereby be made demoniac and deformed.

Up this ladder, into the second cave-world, men and the beings
crowded, following closely the Two Little but Mighty Ones. Yet many
fell back and, lost in the darkness, peopled the under-world, whence
they were delivered in after-time amid terrible earth shakings, becoming the monsters and fearfully strange beings of olden time. Lo! in
this second womb it was dark as is the night of a stormy season, but
larger of space and higher than had been the first, because it was
nearer the navel of the Earth-mother, hence named K'olin tebuli (the
Umbilical-womb, or the Place of Gestation). Here again men and the
beings increased, and the clamour of their complainings grew loud
and beseeching. Again the Two, augmenting the growth of the great
ladder, guided them upward, this time not all at once, but in successive bands to become in time the fathers of the six kinds of men (the
yellow, the tawny grey, the red, the white, the mingled, and the black
races), and with them the gods and creatures of them all. Yet this time
also, as before, multitudes were lost or left behind. The third great
cave-world, where unto men and the creatures had now ascended,
being larger than the second and higher, was lighter, like a valley in
starlight, and named Awisho tehuli—the Vaginal-womb, or the Place
of Sex-generation or Gestation. For here the various peoples and beings
began to multiply apart in kind one from another; and as the nations
and tribes of men and the creatures thus waxed numerous as before,
here, too, it became overfilled. As before, generations of nations now
were led out successively (yet many lost, also as hitherto) into the next
and last world-cave, Tepahaian tehuli, the Ultimate-uncoverable, or
the Womb of Parturition.

Here it was light like the dawning, and men began to perceive and
to learn variously according to their natures, wherefore the Twain
taught them to seek first of all our Sun-father, who would, they said,
reveal to them wisdom and knowledge of the ways of life—wherein
also they were instructing them as we do little children. Yet like the
other cave worlds, this too became, after long time, filled with progeny;
and finally, at periods, the Two led forth the nations of men and the
kinds of being, into this great upper world, which is called Tek'ohaian

ulahnane, or the World of Disseminated Light and Knowledge or Seeing.

F. H. Cushing, *Outlines of Zuñi Creation Myths*, in *Thirteenth Annual Report*, Bureau of Ethnology (Washington, D.C., 1896), pp. 325-447; quotation from pp. 379-83

64. GOD AND THE FIVE WOMEN: A MYTH OF THE ORIGIN OF EARTH, FIRE, WATER AND WOMAN, FROM THE THOMPSON INDIANS OF THE NORTH PACIFIC COAST

Old One or Chief came down from the upper world on a cloud to the surface of the great lake or watery waste which was all that existed. The cloud rested on the lake. Old One pulled five hairs from his head and threw them down: they became five perfectly formed young women. He asked each in turn what she wished to be.

The first replied, 'A woman to bear children. I shall be bad and foolish, and seek after my own pleasure. My descendants will fight, steal, kill, and commit adultery.' The Chief answered that he was sorry, for because of her choice death and trouble would come into the world.

The second replied, 'A woman to bear children. I shall be good and virtuous. My descendants will be wise, peaceful, honest, truthful, and chaste.' The Chief commended her, and said that her way would triumph in the end.

The third chose to become Earth. From her, Old One said, everything would grow, and to her would return at death.

The fourth chose to be Fire, in grass, trees, and all wood, for the good of man. The fifth became Water, to 'cleanse and make wise' the people. 'I will assist all things on earth to maintain life.'

Then the Chief transformed them: first Earth, then Water, then Fire. He placed the two women (good and bad) upon the earth, and impregnated them. He told them they would be the parents of all the people. The evil would be more numerous at first, but the good would prevail eventually, he promised. Then the end will come: all the dead and living will be gathered together, Earth, Fire, and Water will resume their original forms, and all will be transformed and made new.

Condensed and paraphrased from James A. Teit, *Mythology of the Thompson Indians* (Publications of the Jessup North Pacific Expedition, vol. 8, pt. 2 [Leiden and New York: Brill and Stechert, 1912]), pp. 322-4

65. A THOMPSON INDIAN MYTH OF THE CREATION
OF MAN

Before the world was formed, Stars, Moon, Sun, and Earth lived together (as people). Earth was a woman, and Sun was her husband. She was always finding fault with him, saying he was nasty, ugly, and too hot. At last the Sun grew weary of this scolding and left her. The Moon and the Stars went away with him. Earth-Woman was very sad.

The Old One appeared and transformed these people into their present forms. The Sun, Moon, and Stars he assigned to the sky, commanding them never to desert the earth again. Earth-Woman became the solid land: her hair became trees and grass, her flesh clay, her bones rocks, her blood springs of water. 'You will be as the mother of people, for from you their bodies will spring, and to you they will go back. People will live as in your bosom, and sleep on your lap. They will derive nourishment from you, and they will utilize all parts of your body.'

After this the Earth gave birth to people who were very similar in form to ourselves; but they knew nothing and required neither food nor drink. They had no appetites, desires, or thoughts. Then Old One travelled over the world and among the people, giving them appetites and desires. He caused all kinds of birds and fish to appear, to which he gave names and assigned functions. He taught women to make birch baskets, mats, and lodges, and how to dig roots, gather berries, and cure them. He taught men how to make fire, catch fish, trap and shoot game, etc. He instructed couples how to have intercourse and how to give birth to children.

When he had finished teaching the people, he bade them goodbye, saying, 'I now leave you; but if you . . . require my aid, I will come again to you. The Sun is your father, the Earth is your mother's body. You will be covered with her flesh as a blanket, under which your bones will rest in peace.'

Condensed and paraphrased from James A. Teit, *Mythology of the Thompson Indians* (Publications of the Jessup North Pacific Expedition, vol. 8, pt. 2 [Leiden and New York: Brill and Stechert, 1912]), pp. 321-2

66. A PAWNEE EMERGENCE MYTH: MOTHER CORN LEADS
THE FIRST PEOPLE TO THE SURFACE OF THE EARTH

From the ritual account given by the Pawnee Indian, Four Rings, to Dr. Melvin Gilmore.

Before the World was we were all within the Earth.
Mother Corn caused movement. She gave life.
Life being given we moved towards the surface:
We shall stand erect as men!
The being is become human! He is a person!
To personal form is added strength:
Form and intelligence united, we are ready to come forth
But Mother Corn warns us that the Earth is still in flood.
Now Mother Corn proclaims that the flood is gone, and the Earth now green.
Mother Corn commands that the people ascend to the surface.
Mother Corn has gathered them together, they move half way to the surface;
Mother Corn leads them near to the surface of the Earth;
Mother Corn brings them to the surface. The first light appears!
Mother Corn leads them forth. They have emerged to the waist.
They step forth to the surface of the Earth.
Now all have come forth; and Mother Corn leads them from the East towards the West.
Mother Corn leads them to the place of their habitation. . . .
All is completed! All is perfect!

> H. B. Alexander, *The World's Rim* (Lincoln, Neb.: University of Nebraska Press, 1953), p. 89; quoting Dr. Gilmore

67. AN AFRICAN STORY OF THE CREATION OF MAN, FROM THE SHILLUK, A NILOTIC PEOPLE

Turning now to Africa, we find the legend of the creation of mankind out of clay among the Shilluks of the White Nile, who ingeniously explain the different complexions of the various races by the different coloured clays out of which they were fashioned. They say that the creator Juok moulded all men of earth, and that while he was engaged in the work of creation he wandered about the world. In the land of the whites he found a pure white earth or sand, and out of it he shaped white men. Then he came to the land of Egypt and out of the mud of the Nile he made red or brown men. Lastly, he came to the land of the Shilluks, and finding there black earth he created black men out of it. The way in which he modelled men was this. He took a lump of earth and said to himself, 'I will make man, but he must be able to walk and run and go out into the fields, so I will give him two long legs, like the flamingo.' Having done so, he thought again, 'The man must be able to cultivate his millet, so I will give him two arms, one to hold the hoe, and the other to tear up the weeds.' So he gave him two arms. Then he thought again, 'The man must be able to see his millet, so I will give him two eyes.' He did so accordingly. Next he thought to himself, 'The man must be able to eat his millet, so I will give him a mouth.' And a mouth he gave him accordingly. After that he thought within himself, 'The man must be able to dance and speak and sing and shout, and for these purposes he must have a tongue.' And a tongue he gave him accordingly. Lastly, the deity said to himself, 'The man must be able to hear the noise of the dance and the speech of the great men, and for that he needs two ears.' So two ears he gave him, and sent him out into the world a perfect man.'

J. G. Frazer, *Folklore in the Old Testament*, I (London, 1919), pp. 22-3, translating and abridging W. Hofmayr, 'Die Religion der Schilluk,' *Anthropos*, VI (1906), pp. 128 *ff*.

D. MYTHS OF THE ORIGIN OF DEATH

J. G. Frazer distinguished four types of myths of the origin of Death: (1) the type of the Two Messengers; (2) the type of the Waxing and Waning Moon; (3) the type of the Serpent and his Cast Skin; (4) the type of the Banana-tree. Readers will find below examples of the last three types (nos. 68-70). The Aranda myth quoted below (no. 71) illustrates another motif: Death results from the arbitrary and cruel act of a mythical, theriomorphic Being.

The motif of the Two Messengers or 'the message that failed' is especially common in Africa. God sent the chameleon to the mythical ancestors with the message that they would be immortal, and he sent the lizard with the message that they would die. The chameleon sauntered along the way and the lizard arrived first. After she delivered her message, Death entered the world. Another African motif is that of 'Death in a bundle.' God allowed the first human beings to choose between two bundles, one of which contained Life, the other, Death. According to a third African motif, Death is the result of man's transgressing a divine commandment.

68. THE CAST SKIN: A MELANESIAN MYTH

At first men never died, but when they advanced in life they cast their skins like snakes and crabs, and came out with youth renewed. After a time a woman growing old went to a stream to change her skin. She threw off her old skin in the water, and observed that as it floated down it caught against a stick. Then she went home, where she had left her child. The child, however, refused to recognize her, crying that its mother was an old woman not like this young stranger; and to pacify the child she went after her cast integument and put it on. From that time mankind ceased to cast their skins and died.

R. H. Codrington, *The Melanesians* (Oxford, 1891), p. 265

69. THE STONE AND THE BANANA: AN INDONESIAN
MYTH

Thus the natives of Poso, a district of Central Celebes, say that in the beginning the sky was very near the earth, and that the Creator, who lived in it, used to let down his gifts to men at the end of a rope. One day he thus lowered a stone; but our first father and mother would have none of it and they called out to their Maker, 'What have we to do with this stone? Give us something else.' The Creator complied and hauled away at the rope; the stone mounted up and up till it vanished from sight. Presently the rope was seen coming down from heaven again, and this time there was a banana at the end of it instead of a stone. Our first parents ran at the banana and took it. Then there came a voice from heaven saying: 'Because ye have chosen the banana, your life shall be like its life. When the banana-tree has offspring, the parent stem dies; so shall ye die and your children shall step into your place. Had ye chosen the stone, your life would have been like the life of the stone changeless and immortal.' The man and his wife mourned over their fatal choice, but it was too late; that is how through the eating of a banana death came into the world.

J. G. Frazer, *The Belief in Immortality*, I (London, 1913), pp. 74-5, quoting A. C. Kruijt

70. THE MOON AND RESURRECTION: AN AUSTRALIAN
MYTH

In one of the Wotjobaluk legends it is said that at the time when all animals were men and women, some died, and the moon used to say, 'You up-again,' and they came to life again. There was at that time an old man who said, 'Let them remain dead.' Then none ever came to life again, except the moon, which still continued to do so.

A. W. Howitt, *The Native Tribes of South-East Australia* (London, 1904), p. 429

71. THE CRUEL BIRD: AN AUSTRALIAN
(ARANDA TRIBE) MYTH

From a floor of rock they issued forth, south of Ilkanara, from a little rock-hole. The rock was first opened by a curfew woman, who thrust her nose through the hard stone. A second curfew woman followed, then a third, a fourth, a fifth, and so on. And then a curfew man appeared, followed by a second, a third, a fourth, a fifth, and so on to the last. Finally they had all emerged.

The men who had issued forth last all grew angry against the man who had appeared first perhaps because he had followed too closely upon the women. The first-born man lit a great blazing fire; and the others pointed a magic bone at him. The doomed man stretched himself out; he lay motionless for two nights. Then he died, and the rest buried him east of the floor of rock. Some of the women went to Tjolankuta, deep in grief; others went to Lkebalinja; others again sat down at the entrance of the gap where the Ilkaknara creek breaks through the range. They moved about in a women's dance, to the accompaniment of shouts by the men: 'bau! bau! bau! bau!'

But the dead man hollowed out the soil from underneath. Then his forehead emerged through the crust; next his temples reappeared; next his head became visible, up to his throat. His two shoulders, however, had become caught below.

Then the Urbura, the magpie, came from Urburakana. He rushed along in haste; he saw from a great distance away what was happening: 'See, he has begun to sprout up again only a moment ago; but his two shoulders have become caught tightly and are still pinning him down.' The dead man rose a little higher. The curfew women were approaching with dancing steps; they encircled him. The magpie rushed up, filled with deadly anger, to a mountain near-by, called Urburinka. Then he grasped a heavy mulga spear, thrust it deep into the neck of the dead man, stamped him back into the ground with his heel, trampling fiercely upon him: 'Remain rooted down firmly for all time; do not attempt to rise again; stay for ever in the grave!'

Then the curfews all turned into birds and flew to Running Waters; they all left, both men and women. Their wailing shrieks rang out without ceasing; their tears fell without ceasing; they were deeply stricken with grief.

The Urbura, too, soared up like a bird and returned to his own home, where he remained forever.

My informant added briefly that, but for the cruelty of the Urbura, the dead man would have grown up into life a second time; and if he had risen of his own accord, all men who died since that day, would have risen again after death in the same manner. But the Urbura had finally crushed the unfortunate curfew man, and stamped his head down a second time into the grave: 'And now all of us die and are annihilated for ever; and there is no resurrection for us.'

T. G. H. Strehlow, *Aranda Traditions* (Melbourne, 1947), pp. 44-5

72. MAUI AND HINE-NUI-TE-PO: A POLYNESIAN MYTH

Maui now felt it necessary to leave the village where Irawaru had lived, so he returned to his parents. When he had been with them for some time, his father said to him one day, 'Oh, my son, I have heard from your mother and others that you are very valiant, and that you have succeeded in all feats that you have undertaken in your own country, whether they were small or great. But now that you have arrived in your father's country, you will, perhaps, at last be overcome.'

Then Maui asked him, 'What do you mean? What things are there that I can be vanquished by?' His father answered him, 'By your great ancestress, by Hine-nui-te-po, who, if you look, you may see flashing, and, as it were, opening and shutting there, where the horizon meets the sky.' Maui replied, 'Lay aside such idle thoughts, and let us both fearlessly seek whether men are to die or live for ever.' His father said, 'My child, there has been an ill omen for us. When I was baptizing you, I omitted a portion of the fitting prayer, and that I know will be the cause of your perishing.'

Then Maui asked his father, 'What is my ancestress Hine-nui-te-po like?' He answered, 'What you see yonder shining so brightly red are her eyes. And her teeth are as sharp and hard as pieces of volcanic glass. Her body is like that of a man. And as for the pupils of her eyes, they are jasper. And her hair is like the tangles of long seaweed. And her mouth is like that of a barracouta.' Then his son answered him: 'Do you think her strength is as great as that of Tama-nui-te-Ra, who consumes man, and the earth, and the very waters, by the fierceness of his heat? Was not the world formerly saved alive by the speed with which he travelled? If he had then, in the days of his full strength and power, gone as slowly as he does now, not a remnant of mankind would have been left living upon the earth, nor, indeed, would anything else have survived. But I laid hold of Tama-nui-te-Ra, and now he goes slowly, for I smote him again and again, so that he is now feeble, and long in travelling his course, and he now gives but very little heat, having been weakened by the blows of my enchanted weapon. I then, too, split him open in many places, and from the wounds so made, many rays now issue forth and spread in all directions. So, also, I found the sea much larger than the earth, but by the power of the last born of your children, part of the earth was drawn up again, and dry land came forth.' And his father answered him, 'That is all very true, O, my last born, and the strength of my old age. Well, then, be bold, go and visit your great ancestress, who flashes so fiercely there, where the edge of the horizon meets the sky.'

Hardly was this conversation concluded with his father, when the young hero went forth to look for companions to accompany him upon this enterprise. There came to him for companions, the small robin, and the large robin, and the thrush, and the yellow-hammer, and every kind of little bird, and the water-wagtail. These all assembled together, and they all started with Maui in the evening, and arrived at the dwelling of Hine-nui-te-po, and found her fast asleep.

Then Maui addressed them all, 'My little friends, now if you see me creep into this old chieftainess, do not laugh at what you see. Nay, nay, do not, I pray you, but when I have got altogether inside her, and just as I am coming out of her mouth, then you may shout with laughter if you please.' His little friends, who were frightened at what they saw, replied, 'Oh, sir, you will certainly be killed.' He answered them, 'If you burst out laughing at me as soon as I get inside her, you will wake her up, and she will certainly kill me at once, but if you do not laugh until I am quite inside her, and am on the point of coming out of her mouth, I shall live, and Hine-nui-te-po will die.' His little friends answered, 'Go on then, brave sir, but pray take good care of yourself.'

Then the young hero started off. He twisted the strings of his weapon tight round his wrist, and went into the house. He stripped off his clothes, and the skin on his hips looked mottled and beautiful as that of a mackerel, from the tattoo marks, cut on it with the chisel of Uetonga [grandson of Ru, god of earthquakes; Uetonga taught tattooing to Mataora who taught it to man], and he entered the old chieftainess.

The little birds now screwed up their tiny cheeks, trying to suppress their laughter. At last the little Tiwakawaka could no longer keep it in, and laughed out loud, with its merry, cheerful note. This woke the old woman up. She opened her eyes, started up, and killed Maui.

Thus died this Maui we have spoken of. But before he died he had children, and sons were born to him. Some of his descendants yet live in Hawaiki, some in Aotearoa (or in these islands). The greater part of his descendants remained in Hawaiki, but a few of them came here to Aotearoa. According to the traditions of the Maori, this was the cause of the introduction of death into the world (Hine-nui-te-po was the goddess of death. If Maui had passed safely through her, then no more human beings would have died, but death itself would have been destroyed.) We express it by saying, 'The water-wagtail laughing at Maui-tiki-tiki-o Taranga made Hine-nui-te-po squeeze him to death.' And we have this proverb, 'Men make heirs, but death carries them off.'

Sir George Grey, *Polynesian Mythology* (London, 1855), pp. 56-8

E. MYTHS OF THE FLOOD

73. THE FLOOD NARRATIVE FROM THE GILGAMESH EPIC

*Gilgamesh has made a long and difficult journey to learn how Utna-
pishtim acquired eternal life. In answer to his questions, Utnapishtim
tells the following story. Once upon a time, the gods destroyed the
ancient city of Shuruppak in a great flood. But Utnapishtim, fore-
warned by Ea, managed to survive by building a great ship. His
immortality was a gift bestowed by the repentant gods in recognition
of his ingenuity and his faithfulness in reinstituting the sacrifice.*

> Shurippak—a city which thou knowest,
> (And) which on Euphrates' banks is set—
> That city was ancient, (as were) the gods within it,
> When their heart led the great gods to produce the flood.
> There were Anu, their father,
> Valiant Enlil, their counsellor,
> Ninurta, their herald,
> Ennuge, their irrigator.
> Ninigiku-Ea was also present with them;
> Their words he repeats to the reed-hut:[1]
> 'Reed-hut, reed-hut! Wall! Wall!
> Reed-hut, hearken! Wall, reflect!
> Man of Shuruppak,[2] son of Ubar-Tutu,
> Tear down (this) house, build a ship!
> Give up possessions, seek thou life.
> Despise property and keep the soul alive.
> Aboard the ship take thou the seed of all living things.
> The ship that thou shalt build,
> Her dimensions shall be to measure.
> Equal shall be her width and her length.
> Like the Apsu[3] thou shalt ceil her.'

I understood, and I said to Ea, my lord:
'Behold, my lord, what thou hast thus ordered,
I shall be honoured to carry out.
But what shall I answer the city, the people and elders?'
Ea opened his mouth to speak,
Saying to me, his servant:
'Thou shalt then thus speak unto them:
"I have learned that Enlil is hostile to me,
So that I cannot reside in your city,
Nor set my foot in Enlil's territory.
To the Deep I will therefore go down,
   To dwell with my lord Ea.
But upon you he will shower down abundance,
The choicest birds, the rarest fishes.
The land shall have its fill of harvest riches.
He who at dusk orders the husk-greens,
Will shower down upon you a rain of wheat." '[4]
With the first glow of dawn,
The land was gathered about me.

   [too fragmentary for translation]

The little ones carried bitumen,
While the grown ones brought all else that was needful.
On the fifth day I laid her framework.
One (whole) acre was her floor space,
   Ten dozen cubits the height of each of her walls,
Ten dozen cubits each edge of the square deck.
I laid out the shape of her sides and joined her together.
I provided her with six decks,
Dividing her (thus) into seven parts.
Her floor plan I divided into nine parts.
I hammered water-plugs into her.
I saw to the punting-poles and laid in supplies.
Six 'sar' (measures)[5] of bitumen I poured into the furnace,
Three sar of asphalt I also poured inside.
Three sar of the basket-bearers transferred,
Aside from the one sar of oil which the calking consumed,
And the two sar of oil which the boatman stowed away.
Bullocks I slaughtered for the people,
And I killed sheep every day.
Must, red wine, oil, and white wine

Myths of the Flood

I gave the workmen to drink, as though river water,
That they might feast as on New Year's Day. . . .
On the seventh day the ship was completed.
The launching was very difficult,
So that they had to shift the floor planks above and below,
Until two-thirds of the structure had gone into the water.
Whatever I had I laded upon her:
Whatever I had of silver I laded upon her;
Whatever I had of gold I laded upon her;
Whatever I had of all the living beings I laded upon her.
All my family and kin I made go aboard the ship.
The beasts of the field, the wild creatures of the field,
    All the craftsmen I made go aboard.
Shamash had set for me a stated time:
'When he who orders unease at night
    Will shower down a rain of blight,
Board thou the ship and batten up the gate!'
That stated time had arrived:
'He who orders unease at night showers down a rain of blight.'
I watched the appearance of the weather.
The weather was awesome to behold.
I boarded the ship and battened up the gate.
To batten up the (whole) ship, to Puzur-Amurri, the boatman,
I handed over the structure together with its contents.
With the first glow of dawn,
A black cloud rose up from the horizon.
Inside it Adad[6] thunders,
While Shallat and Hanish[7] go in front,
Moving as heralds over hill and plain.
Erragal[8] tears out the posts;[9]
Forth comes Ninurta and causes the dikes to follow.
The Anunnaki lift up the torches,
Setting the land ablaze with their glare.
Consternation over Adad reaches to the heavens,
Turning to blackness all that had been light.
The wide land was shattered like a pot!
For one day the south-storm blew,
Gathering speed as it blew, submerging the mountains,
Overtaking the people like a battle.
No one can see his fellow,
Nor can the people be recognized from heaven.

The gods were frightened by the deluge,
And, shrinking back, they ascended to the heaven of Anu.
The gods cowered like dogs
*   Crouched against the outer wall.*
Ishtar cried out like a woman in travail,
The sweet-voiced mistress of the gods moans aloud:
'The olden days are alas turned to clay,
Because I bespoke evil in the Assembly of the gods,
How could I bespeak evil in the Assembly of the gods,
Ordering battle for the destruction of my people,
When it is I myself who give birth to my people!
Like the spawn of the fishes they fill the sea!'
The Anunnaki gods weep with her,
The gods, all humbled, sit and weep,
Their lips drawn tight, . . . one and all.
Six days and six nights
Blows the flood wind, as the south-storm sweeps the land.
When the seventh day arrived,
*   The flood (-carrying) south-storm subsided in the battle,*
Which it had fought like an army.
The sea grew quiet, the tempest was still, the flood ceased.
I looked at the weather: stillness had set in,
And all of mankind had returned to clay.
The landscape was as level as a flat roof.
I opened a hatch, and light fell on my face.
Bowing low, I sat and wept,
Tears running down my face.
I looked about for coast lines in the expanse of the sea:
In each of fourteen (regions)
*   There emerged a region (-mountain).*
On Mount Nisir the ship came to a halt.
Mount Nisir held the ship fast,
*   Allowing no motion.*

....

[For six days the ship is held fast by Mount Nisir.]

When the seventh day arrived,
I sent forth and set free a dove.
The dove went forth, but came back;
There was no resting-place for it and she turned round.
Then I sent forth and set free a swallow.

148

The swallow went forth, but came back;
There was no resting-place for it and she turned round.
Then I sent forth and set free a raven.
The raven went forth and, seeing that the waters had diminished,
He eats, circles, caws, and turns not round.
Then I let out (all) to the four winds
   And offered a sacrifice.
I poured out a libation on the top of the mountain.
Seven and seven cult-vessels I set up,
Upon their plate-stands I heaped cane, cedarwood, and myrtle.
The gods smelled the savour,
The gods smelled the sweet savour,
The gods crowded like flies about the sacrificer.
As soon as the great goddess[10] arrived,
She lifted up the great jewels which Anu had fashioned to her liking:
'Ye gods here, as surely as this lapis
   Upon my neck I shall not forget,
I shall be mindful of these days, forgetting (them) never.
Let the gods come to the offering:
(But) let not Enlil come to the offering,
For he, unreasoning, brought on the deluge
And my people consigned to destruction.'
As soon as Enlil arrived,
And saw the ship, Enlil was wroth,
He was filled with wrath against the Igigi gods:[11]
'Has some living soul escaped?
   No man was to survive the destruction!'
Ninurta opened his mouth to speak,
   Saying to valiant Enlil:
'Who other than Ea can devise plans?
It is Ea alone who knows every matter.'
Ea opened his mouth to speak,
   Saying to valiant Enlil:
'Thou wisest of the gods, thou hero,
How couldst thou, unreasoning, bring on the deluge?
On the sinner impose his sin,
   On the transgressor impose his transgression!
(Yet) be lenient, lest he be cut off,
Be patient, lest he be dislodged!
Instead of thy bringing on the deluge,
   Would that a lion had risen up to diminish mankind!

Instead of thy brining on the deluge,
  Would that a wolf had risen up to diminish mankind!
Instead of thy bringing on the deluge,
  Would that a famine had risen up to lay low mankind!
Instead of thy bringing on the deluge,
  Would that pestilence had risen up to smite down mankind!
It was not I who disclosed the secret of the great gods.
I let Atrahasis[12] see a dream,
And he perceived the secret of the gods.
Now then take counsel in regard to him!'
Thereupon Enlil went aboard the ship.
Holding me by the hand, he took me aboard.
He took my wife aboard and made (her) kneel by my side.
Standing between us, he touched our foreheads to bless us:
'Hitherto Utnapishtim has been but human.
Henceforth Utnapishtim and his wife shall be like unto us gods.
Utnapishtim shall reside far away, at the mouth of the rivers!'
Thus they took me and made me reside far away,
  At the mouth of the rivers.

Notes

1 Probably the dwelling of Utnapishtim. The god Ea addresses him (through the barrier of the wall), telling him about the decision of the gods to bring on a flood and advising him to build a ship.
2 Utnapishtim.
3 The subterranean waters.
4 The purpose is to deceive the inhabitants of Shuruppak as to the real intent of the rain.
5 A 'sar' is about 8,000 gallons.
6 God of storm and rain.
7 Heralds of Adad.
8 I.e., Nergal, the god of the nether world.
9 Of the world dam.
10 Ishtar.
11 The heavenly gods.
12 'Exceeding wise,' an epithet of Utnapishtim.

Translation by E. A. Speiser, in *Ancient Near Eastern Texts* (Princeton, 1950), pp. 60-72, as reprinted in Isaac Mendelsohn (ed.), *Religions of the Ancient Near East*, Library of Religion paperbook series (New York, 1955), pp. 100-6; notes by Mendelsohn

See also no. 159

74. A MYTH OF THE DELUGE FROM ANCIENT INDIA

('Shatapatha-Brāhmana,' 1, 8, 1-6)

1. In the morning they brought to Manu water for washing, just as now also they (are wont to) bring (water) for washing the hands. When he was washing himself, a fish came into his hands.

2. It spake to him the word, 'Rear me, I will save thee!' 'Wherefrom wilt thou save me?' 'A flood will carry away all these creatures: from that I will save thee!' 'How am I to rear thee?'

3. It said, 'As long as we are small, there is great destruction for us: fish devours fish. Thou wilt first keep me in a jar. When I outgrow that, thou wilt dig a pit and keep me in it. When I outgrow that, thou wilt take me down to the sea, for then I shall be beyond destruction.'

4. It soon became a *ghasha* (a great fish); for that grows largest (of all fish). Thereupon it said, 'In such and such a year that flood will come. Thou shalt then attend to me (i.e. to my advice) by preparing a ship; and when the flood has risen thou shalt enter into the ship, and I will save thee from it.'

5. After he had reared it in this way, he took it down to the sea. And in the same year which the fish had indicated to him, he attended to (the advice of the fish) by preparing a ship; and when the flood had risen, he entered into the ship. The fish then swam up to him, and to its horn he tied the rope of the ship, and by that means he passed swiftly up to yonder northern mountain.

6. It then said, 'I have saved thee. Fasten the ship to a tree; but let not the water cut thee off whilst thou art on the mountain. As the water subsides, thou mayest gradually descend!' Accordingly he gradually descended and hence that (slope) of the northern mountain is called 'Manu's descent.' The flood then swept away all these creatures, and Manu alone remained here.

Translation by Julius Eggeling, *in Sacred Books of the East*, XII (Oxford, 1882), pp. 216-18

Acknowledgments

Bibliography

Index

ACKNOWLEDGMENTS

Acknowledgment is made to the following for permission to reprint copyrighted material:

THE ADMINISTRATION OF SOUTH WEST AFRICA for extract from 'The Herero' by Heinrich Vedder, in *The Native Tribes of Southwest Africa;* published with the kind permission of the Administration of South West Africa.

GEORGE ALLEN AND UNWIN, LTD for extracts from *The Koran,* translated by A. J. Arberry.

THE AMERICAN MUSEUM OF NATURAL HISTORY for extract from *The Sun Dance and Other Ceremonies of the Oglala Division of the Teton Dakota* by J. R. Walker, reprinted by courtesy of the American Museum of Natural History.

THE AMERICAN-SCANDINAVIAN FOUNDATION for extracts from *The Poetic Edda,* translated by Henry Adams Bellows.

THE ASIATIC SOCIETY OF JAPAN for extract from *Kojiki,* Supplement to Transactions of the Asiatic Society of Japan x (1906), translated by B. H. Chamberlain, reprinted by permission of the Asiatic Society of Japan.

BERNICE P. BISHOP MUSEUM for extracts from *Polynesian Religion* by E. S. Craighill Handy, Honolulu: Bernice P. Bishop Museum (Bulletin 34), 1927, quoted with permission.

BOLLINGEN FOUNDATION for extracts from *Hindu Polytheism* by Alain Daniélou, Bollingen Series LXXIII, pp. 367-8 and 377-9, Pantheon Books; and *Monotheism among Primitive Peoples* by Paul Radin, Special Publications of the Bollingen Foundation no. 4 (also issued by the Ethnographical Museum, Basel, Switzerland, 1954), pp. 13, 14, 15, Pantheon Books.

BRUNO CASSIRER (PUBLISHERS) LTD for extracts from *Buddhist Texts Through the Ages* edited by Edward Conze (1954).

CATHOLIC UNIVERSITY OF AMERICA PRESS for extracts from *The Apinaye* by Curt Nimuendaju.

THE CLARENDON PRESS, OXFORD for extracts from *Hymns of the Atharva Veda,* translated by M. Bloomfield; *A Vedic Reader for Students* by A. A. Macdonnell; *Zurvan* by R. C. Zaehner; all are reprinted by permission of the Clarendon Press, Oxford.

COLUMBIA UNIVERSITY PRESS for extracts from *Sources of Japanese Tradition,* edited by William Theodore de Bary, copyright © 1958 by Columbia University Press, New York.

COOPER SQUARE PUBLISHERS, INC for extracts from *Latin American Mythology* by H. B. Alexander.

EDINBURGH HOUSE PRESS for extracts from *African Ideas of God* by Edwin W. Smith.

FUNK & WAGNALLS, N.Y. for extract from *The Beginning: Creation Myths around the World,* reprinted by permission of the publishers, Funk and Wagnalls, N. Y.

GOEMAERE PUBLISHERS for extract from *Etudes Bakongo* by S. J. Van Wing, as

Acknowledgments

translated by Edwin W. Smith, *African Ideas of God.*

HARVARD UNIVERSITY PRESS for extracts from *Bhagavad Gītā,* vol. I, Oriental Series, vol. 38, translated and interpreted by Franklin Edgerton (1944).

HARVARD UNIVERSITY PRESS and THE LOEB CLASSICAL LIBRARY for extracts from Apollodorus, *The Library,* vol. I, translated by Sir James G. Frazer; *Herodotus,* vol. II, translated by A. D. Godley; Hesiod, *The Homeric Hymns and Homerica,* translated by Hugh G. Evelyn-White; all are reprinted by permission of the publishers and The Loeb Classical Library.

THE INTERNATIONAL AFRICAN INSTITUTE and Jomo Kenyatta, for extract from 'Kikuyu Religion, Ancestor-Worship and Sacrificial Practices', *Africa,* vol. X (1937); James W. Telch, for extract from 'The Isoko Tribe', *Africa,* vol. III (1934).

LIBERAL ARTS DIVISION OF THE BOBBS-MERRILL COMPANY INC. for extracts from *Hesiod's Theogony,* translated by Norman O. Brown, copyright © 1953 by the Liberal Arts Press.

THE MACMILLAN COMPANY for extracts from *The Koran,* translated by A. J. Arberry.

MACMILLAN AND CO. LTD, LONDON for extract from *The Ila-Speaking People of Northern Rhodesia* by E. W. Smith and A. M. Dale. Copyright © 1955 by Allen & Unwin, Ltd.

JOHN MURRAY for extracts from *The Hymns of Zarathustra,* translated by J. Duchesne-Guillemin.

MUSEUM OF THE AMERICAN INDIAN for extract from *Religion and Ceremonies of the Lenape* by M. R. Harrington.

THOMAS NELSON & SONS LTD for extracts from *Documents from Old Testament Times* edited by D. Winton Thomas (1958).

OXFORD UNIVERSITY PRESS, LONDON for extracts from *The Bavenda* by H. A. Stayt (as quoted in Edwin W. Smith, *African Ideas of God*), published by the Oxford University Press under the auspices of the International African Institute.

THE POLYNESIAN SOCIETY (INC), WELLINGTON, NEW ZEALAND for extracts from 'A Maori Cosmogony' by Hare Hongi, *Journal of the Polynesian Society,* vol. XVI, 1907; 'Maori Personifications' by Elsdon Best, *Journal of the Polynesian Society,* vol. XXXII, (1923).

PRINCETON UNIVERSITY PRESS for extracts from *Ancient Near Eastern Texts Relating to the Old Testament,* edited by James B. Pritchard, reprinted by permission of the Princeton University Press, Copyright 1950.

SIDGWICK AND JACKSON LTD for extracts from *The Wonder that Was India* by A. L. Basham, reprinted by permission of the author's representatives and of the publishers Sidgwick and Jackson Ltd.

T. G. H. STREHLOW for extract from his *Aranda Traditions,* published by Melbourne University Press.

THAMES AND HUDSON LTD for extracts from *Myth and Symbol in Ancient Egypt* by R. T. Rundle Clark.

TRINITY COLLEGE, CAMBRIDGE for extracts from *The Belief in Immortality,* vol. I by James G. Frazer, published by Macmillan and Co. Ltd and *Folklore in the Old Testament* by James G. Frazer, published by Macmillan and Co. Ltd.

THE UNIVERSITY OF CALIFORNIA PRESS for extracts from *Indian Myths of South Central California* by A. L. Kroeber (University of California Publications in American Archaeology, vol. IV, no. 4, 1906-1907).

Acknowledgments

THE UNIVERSITY OF CHICAGO PRESS for extracts from *The Sumerians* by Samuel N. Kramer.

THE UNIVERSITY OF NEBRASKA PRESS for extracts reprinted from *The World's Rim* by Hartley Burr Alexander by permission of University of Nebraska Press, copyright 1953, University of Nebraska Press, Lincoln, Nebraska.

THE UNIVERSITY OF OKLAHOMA PRESS for extracts from *Naskapi: the Savage Hunters of the Labrador Peninsula,* by Frank G. Speck, copyright 1935 by the University of Oklahoma Press.

BIBLIOGRAPHY

Chapter 1: *Gods, Goddesses, and Supernatural Beings*

No. 1. On the 'primitive' Supreme Beings and High Gods, see the bibliographies listed in M. Eliade, *Patterns in Comparative Religion*, trans. Rosemary Sheed (London and New York: Sheed and Ward, 1958; Meridian paperbook, 1963), pp. 112-16. On the Australian materials, see Raffaele Pettazzoni, *Dio*, vol. I, titled *L'essere celeste nelle credenze dei popoli primitivi* (Rome, 1922), pp. 1-40; Raffaele Pettazzoni, *The All-Knowing God*, trans. H. J. Rose (London, 1955), chap. XXI; Wilhelm Schmidt, *Der Ursprung der Gottesidee*, vol. III (Münster, 1931), passim; A. P. Elkin, *The Australian Aborigines*, 3rd ed.; (Sydney, 1959; Doubleday Anchor Book, 1964). pp. 196 *ff.*; W. E. A. Stanner, 'On Aboriginal Religion,' *Oceania*, XXX (1959), nos. 2 and 4; XXXI (1960), nos. 2 and 4; XXXII (1961), no. 20.

Nos. 1ff. On African materials, see Raffaele Pettazzoni, *Dio*, *op. cit.*, pp. 186-259; Raffaele Pettazzoni, *Miti e Leggende*, vol. I (Africa, Australia), pp. 3-401; Raffaele Pettazzoni, *The All-Knowing God* (London, 1955), chap. I; Wilhelm Schmidt, *Ursprung der Gottesidee*, vol. IV (Münster, 1933), vol. VII (Münster, 1941), and vol. VIII (Münster, 1949); J. G. Frazer, *The Worship of Nature* (London, 1926), pp. 89-315; Edwin W. Smith (ed.), *African Ideas of God: A Symposium* (London, 1950); and the bibliographies listed in M. Eliade, *Patterns in Comparative Religion*, trans. Rosemary Sheed (New York and London: Sheed and Ward, 1958), pp. 113-14.

Nos. 8ff. On North and South America, see bibliographies in M. Eliade, *Patterns in Comparative Religion*, pp. 114-15; Wilhelm Schmidt, *Ursprung der Gottesidee*, vols II and V (Münster, 1937); Wilhelm Schmidt, *High Gods in North America* (Oxford, 1933); Raffaele Pettazzoni, *Dio*, pp. 260-348; Raffaele Pettazzoni, *The All-Knowing God*, chaps. XXII-XXIV; Raffaele Pettazzoni, *Miti e Leggende*, vol. III (North America), IV (Central and South America).

No. 13. On the Sun Gods, see bibliographies in M. Eliade, *Patterns in Comparative Religion*, *op. cit.*, pp. 152-3; J. G. Frazer, *The Worship of Nature* (London, 1926), pp. 441-667.

No. 14. On the master of animals, see Raffaele Pettazzoni, *The All-Knowing God* (London 1955), pp. 440 *ff.*; John M. Cooper, *The Northern Algonquian Supreme Being* (Washington D.C., 1934); Otto Zerries, *Wild-und-Buschgeister in Südamerika* (Stuttgart, 1954); Ake Hultkrantz, 'The Owner of the Animals in the Religion of the North American Indians,' *The Supernatural Owners of Nature*, ed. A. Hultkrantz (Stockholm, 1961), pp. 53-64; Ivar Paulson, *Schultzgeister und Gottheiten des Wildes (Der Jagdtiere und Fische) in Nordeurasien* (Stockholm, 1961); I. Paulson, 'The Animal Guardian: A Critical and Synthetic Review, *History of Religions*, III (1964), pp. 202-19.

Bibliography

No. 15. On Hainuwele and the *Dema*-deities, see A. E. Jensen, *Hainuwele: Volkserzählungen von der Molukkeninsel Ceram* (Frankfurt, 1939); A. E. Jensen, *Das religiöse Weltbild einer frühen Kultur* (Stuttgart, 1948); A. E. Jensen, *Myth and Cult among Primitive Peoples*, trans. Marianna Tax Choldin and Wolfgang Weissleder (Chicago, 1963); Joseph Campbell, *The Masks of God: Primitive Mythology* (New York, 1959), pp. 173 *ff.*, 188 *ff.*

No. 17. On Egyptian religions, see the bibliographies in Jacques Vandier, *La Religion Egyptienne* (Paris, 1944), pp. 1-9; also Hans Bonnet, *Reallexikon der Ägyptischen Religionsgeschichte* (Berlin, 1952); Henri Frankfort, *Ancient Egyptian Religion* (New York, Harper Torchbook, 1961); R. T. Rundle Clark, *Myth and Symbol in Ancient Egypt* (London, 1959; New York, 1960); Wolfgang Helkck, *Die Mythologie de alten Ägypter* (in *Wörterbuch der Mythologie*, ed. H. W. Hausig, vol. I, *Die Alten Kulturvölker*), pp. 315-406.

Nos. 21 *ff.* On the Indian (Vedic and Brahmanic) religious texts available in English translations see the bibliographies compiled by Norwin J. Hein, 'Hinduism,' in Charles J. Adams (ed.), *A Reader's Guide to the Great Religions, op. cit.*, pp. 46 *ff.* On the *Bhagavad Gītā* and Krishna worship, Adams (ed.), pp. 62 *ff.* A considerable number of texts are translated by Alain Daniélou, *Hindu Polytheism* (New York, 1964).

For a bibliography of the English translations of Buddhist texts, see Richard A. Gard, 'Buddhism,' in Adams (ed.), *A Reader's Guide to the Great Religions, op. cit.*, pp. 111 *ff.* A select list in Edward Conze, *Buddhism: Its Essence and Development* (Oxford, 1951; Harper Torchbook, 1959), pp. 225-6.

No. 29. Cf. *The Lotus of the Wonderful Law*, translated by W. Soothill (1930).

No. 30. Har Dayal, *The Boddhisattva Doctrine in Buddhist Sanskrit Literature* (London, 1932); cf. Adams (ed.), *A Reader's Guide to the Great Religions, op. cit.*, p. 148.

No. 31. On the Japanese gods, see the bibliographies compiled by Joseph M. Kitagawa, 'The Religions of Japan,' in Adams (ed.), *A Reader's Guide to the Great Religions, op. cit.*, pp. 168-9.

Nos. 32 *ff.* On the Greek Gods, see W. K. C. Guthrie, *The Greeks and Their Gods* (London, 1950; Beacon paperbook, 1955); Walter F. Otto, *The Homeric Gods*, trans. Moses Hadas (1954; Beacon paperbook, 1964).

No. 36. On Zalmoxis, see Carl Clement, 'Zalmoxis,' *Zalmoxis. Revue des Etudes Religieuses*, II (Paris-Bucharest, 1939), pp. 53-62; Karl Meuli, 'Scythica,' *Hermes*, LXX (1935), pp. 127-76, esp. pp. 162 *ff.*; R. Pettazzoni, 'Il "monoteismo" dei Geti,' *Studia in Honorem Acad. D. Decev* (Sofia, 1958), pp. 649-55.

Nos. 37-9. On the translations of the *Gathas*, see R. C. Zaehner, *The Dawn and Twilight of Zoroastrianism* (London, 1961), pp. 340-1. We made use of J. Duchesne-Guillemin's translation, *The Hymns of Zoroaster* (London, 1952; Beacon Paperbook, 1963). A critical bibliography of the texts and their interpretations by various scholars, in J. Duchesne-Guillemin, *La Religion de l'Iran ancien* (Paris, 1962), pp. 17-70. Cf. also Georges Dumézil, *Naissance d'archanges* (Paris, 1945; G. Dumézil, *Les dieux des Indo-Européens* (Paris, 1952); G. Dumézil, *L'idéologie tripartie des Indo-Européens* (Bruxelles, 1958).

On Iranian religions in general, see R. C. Zaehner, *The Dawn and Twilight, op. cit.*; R. C. Zaehner *Zurvan, : A Zoroastrian Dilemma* (Oxford, 1955); J. Duchesne-Guillemin, *La Religion de l'Iran ancien, op. cit.*; J. Duchesne-Guillemin, *Symbols and Values in Zoroastrianism* (New York, 1966); George

Bibliography

Widengren, *Die Religionen Irans* (Stuttgart, 1965), pp. 360-75, bibliography; G. Widengren, *Iranische Geisteswelt* (Baden-Baden, 1961).

Nos. 40 *ff*. On the Prophet Muhammad and his biographies, see the critical bibliographies in Charles J. Adams, 'Islam,' in his *A Reader's Guide to the Great Religions*, pp. 293-9. On the translations of the Koran, see Adams (ed.), *op. cit.*, pp. 300-1. On the critical works on the Koran, see Adams (ed.), *op. cit.*, pp. 302-5.

The most readable biography in English is Tor Andrae's *Mohammed: The Man and His Faith* (trans. Theophil Menze, New York, 1935; Harper Torchbook, 1960). For a more meticulous study, cf. W. Montgomery Watt, *Muhammad at Mecca* (Oxford, 1953) and *Muhammad at Medina* (Oxford, 1956).

Chapter 11: *Myths of Creation and of Origin*

Nos. 44 *ff*. On the different types of cosmogonical myths, see Charles H. Long, *Alpha: The Myths of Creation* (New York, 1963) and the bibliography listed on pp. 248-51; S. G. F. Brandon, *Creation Legends of the Ancient Near East* (London, 1963); *La naissance du monde* (Collection 'Sources Orientales' [Paris, 1959]; translations of cosmogonic texts from the Ancient Near East, India, Iran, Tibet, China, Laos, Siam); cf. F. Lukas, *Die Grundbegriffe in den Kosmogonien der alten Völker* (Leipzig, 1893); A. Kuhn, *Berichte über den Weltanfang bei den Indochinesen und ihren Nachbarvölkern* (Leipzig, 1935); W. Münsterberger, *Ethnologische Studien an Indonesischen Schöpfungsmythen* (The Hague, 1939); H. Baumann, *Das doppelte Geschlecht* (Berlin, 1955), pp. 164 *ff*., 184 *ff*., 268 *ff*.; Anna-Britta Helbom, 'The Creation Egg,' *Ethnos*, XXVIII (1963), pp. 63-105. See also Raffaele Pettazzoni, *Essays on the History of Religions* (Leiden, 1954), pp. 24 *ff*. On 'Myths of Beginnings and Creation-Myths'; M. Eliade, *Myth and Reality* (New York, 1963), pp. 1-74.

No. 49. On the earth-diver motif, see M. Eliade, 'Le plongeon cosmogonique,' *Revue de l'Histoire des Religions*, CIX (1961), pp. 157-212.

No. 53. On Japanese mythological and cosmological traditions, see the bibliography of Joseph M. Kitagawa, 'The Religions of Japan' in Adams (ed.), *A Reader's Guide to the Great Religions*, *op. cit.*, pp. 175 *ff*. For a comparative study, cf. F. K. Numazawa, *Die Weltanfänge in der japanischen Mythologie* (Paris-Luzern, 1946).

No. 54. On Egyptian creation myths, see the bibliography listed in Serge Sauneron and Jean Yoyotte, 'La naissance du monde selon l'Egypte Ancienne,' *La naissance du monde*, *op. cit.*, pp. 88 *ff*.

No. 55. On Babylonian cosmogony, see Alexander Heidel, *The Babylonian Genesis* (Chicago, 1954).

No. 59. On Hesiod's cosmogonic myth, see introduction (pp. 7-48) and bibliography (p. 49) of *Hesiod's Theogony*, trans. Norman O. Brown (New York, 1953). Cf. also W. Staudacher, *Die Trennung von Himmel und Erde. Ein vorgriechischer Schöpfungsmythus bei Hesiod und die Orphikern* (Tübingen, 1942).

No. 60. On Iranian cosmogony, cf. Jacques Duchesne-Guillemin, *La Religion de l'Iran ancien* (Paris, 1962), pp. 207 *ff*.

Bibliography

No. 61. On the *Völuspá*, see Jan de Vries, *Altgermanische Religionsgeschichte*, vol. II (2nd ed.; Berlin, 1957), pp. 359 *ff*.

Nos. 62 *ff*. On the creation of man, see the materials collected by J. G. Frazer, *Folklore in the Old Testament*, vol. I (London, 1919), pp. 3-44.

Nos. 68 *ff*. On myths of the origin of death, see J. G. Frazer, *Folklore in the Old Testament, op. cit.*, vol. I, pp. 45-77; Hans Abrahamsson, *The Origin of Death: Studies in African Mythology*, Studia Ethnographica Upsaliensia, III (Uppsala, 1951).

Nos. 73-4. On the Flood narrative from the *Gilgamesh Epic*, see Alexander Heidel, *The Gilgamesh Epic and Old Testament Parallels* (Chicago, 1946). On myths of the Great Flood, see J. G. Frazer, *Folklore in the Old Testament, op. cit.*, vol. I, pp. 104-361.

ETHNIC AND GEOGRAPHIC
CROSS-REFERENCE INDEX

Ancient Europe

Getae: no. 36
Greeks: nos. 32, 33, 34, 35, 59
Scandinavians: no. 61

Ancient Near East

Egypt: nos. 17, 18, 19, 20, 54
Iran: nos. 37, 38, 39, 60
Mesopotamia: nos. 16, 55, 73

Asia

Ancient India: Brahmanism, Hinduism, Vedism
  Bhagavad Gītā: no. 28
  The Laws of Manu: no. 74
  Purānās: no. 27
  Vedic hymns: nos. 21, 22, 23, 24, 25, 26, 56, 57, 58
Buddhism: nos. 29, 30
Islam: nos. 40, 41, 42, 43
Japan: nos. 31, 53

Primitives (Pre-literate Societies)

Africa: nos. 2, 3, 4, 5, 6, 7, 51, 67
Asia: nos. 69
Australia: nos. 1, 70, 71
North, Central, and South America: nos. 8, 9, 10, 12, 13, 14, 44, 45, 46, 49, 50, 52, 63, 64, 65, 66
Oceania: nos. 11, 15, 47, 48, 62, 68, 72

74 75 76 77 10 9 8 7 6 5 4 3 2 1